goof-Proof Skits for youtH ministry

by
John Duckworth

Group
Loveland, Colorado

Dedication
To Christopher and Jonathan, my favorite comedy team.

NOTE:

The price of this text includes the right for you to make as many copies of the skits as you need for your immediate church performing group. If another church or organization wants copies of these skits, it must purchase *Goof-Proof Skits for Youth Ministry* in order to receive performance rights.

Credits
Book Acquisitions Editor: Mike Nappa
Editor: Steve Parolini
Senior Editor: Dan Benson
Creative Products Director: Joani Schultz
Copy Editor: Sandra Collier
Art Director: Helen Lannis
Cover Art Director: Liz Howe
Designer and Illustrator: DeWain Stoll
Computer Graphic Artist: Joyce Douglas
Illustrator: Bron Smith
Production Manager: Gingar Kunkel and Ann Marie Gordon

Unless otherwise noted, Scriptures quoted from The Youth Bible, New Century Version, copyright © 1991 by Word Publishing, Dallas, Texas 75039. Used by permission.

Library of Congress Cataloging-in-Publication Data
Duckworth, John (John L.)
    Goof-proof skits for youth ministry / by John Duckworth.
       p.   cm.
    Includes indexes.
    ISBN 1-55945-795-3
    1. Drama in Christian education. 2. Church work with teenagers. 3. Amateur plays. I. Title.
BV1534.4.D829   1995
246' .7–dc20   95-17207
                                     CIP

10 9 8 7 6 5 4 3   04 03 02 01 00 99 98 97 96
Printed in the United States of America.

Contents

Introduction

Welcome to the Skit Book for *Every* Group!

Sure, skits are a great idea for youth ministry. They make learning active and visual. They build relationships as kids learn to work together. They brighten meetings with humor while driving home important points.

But only if your kids can *act*.

If your group is like most—that is, if it's not composed entirely of drama-club presidents and speech-team captains—your experience with skits may be nothing to write home about. If some of your kids are "theatrically challenged," you may find yourself avoiding skits entirely or using the same few talented kids over and over.

Your dilemma: Should you keep less-skilled members of your group off the stage, making them feel left out? Or should you use everybody and limp through some ineffective and embarrassing efforts?

Would you like a third choice? How about trying *Goof-Proof Skits for Youth Ministry*?

Real Fun, Real Truths—for Real Kids.

What do you want in a skit? Fun? It's here—from pratfalls to parables to TV-show parodies. Solid, Bible-based messages? They're here, too—on important topics such as love and sex, missions, and racism.

But you get even more with *Goof-Proof Skits for Youth Ministry*. You get *help* to make each skit *work*.

Every script in this book has been prepared with *real* kids in mind. You'll find no page-long speeches to stumble through, no delicate emotional nuances to steamroll, no split-second timing to fumble. The language is simple—the feelings straightforward.

Best of all, *Goof-Proof Skits for Youth Ministry* gives you innovative cues to help draw the best possible reading—and the most meaning—from every line of dialogue. Each script features simple facial-expression symbols to show kids instantly how to put the right feeling into each line. We've also put in all capital letters the words that should be spoken with emphasis. This helps to beat the "monotone syndrome" and ensures that everyone catches key concepts.

The result? Skits that build confidence. Skits that let you cast practically anybody. Skits that cut mistakes to a minimum so that the message can't miss. Skits that work in any group—dramatically inclined or not.

Goof-Proof Skits for Youth Ministry may not turn your kids into Tony award winners. But when it comes to getting all your kids involved—and getting the message across ungarbled—you'll find no better or easier way than with this book.

Use it in your youth meetings, retreats, Sunday school, Bible studies, worship services—with or without rehearsal—whenever you want to make a point in a fresh, funny, memorable way. With each script you'll find Scriptures to study, a relevant topic to explore, easy setup ideas, thought-provoking discussion questions, and optional extras. You'll find so much, in fact, that you can turn each skit into a complete youth group session of its own—if you want to.

And After the Skit?

Youth ministry doesn't end when the skit's over—so the skits in this book don't end there either. You can take advantage of the discussion questions provided in the "For Post-Play Pondering" section to help your kids dig deeper into the skit topics.

As you lead kids in post-play pondering, remember that variety and interaction help make discussions exciting for teenagers. Use large groups, small groups, pairs, and trios. Or have kids number off from one to five, then have all the ones respond to the first question, all the twos respond to the second, and so on. Or have kids write their own questions about the topic based on what they saw in the skit. The possibilities are endless!

A great skit can be one of your most powerful tools for helping teenagers grow in faith—if it works. The goof-proof skits and post-play ponderings in this book are your chance to get more of that dramatic power off the page—and into the hearts of your group members.

Key to Expression Symbols

To help group members know at a glance how to say their lines, the dialogue in this book includes simple facial-expression symbols. Most kids will grasp quickly the emotions represented by the symbols, so you shouldn't need to explain them. For *your* reference, though, here are the *official* meanings of those little faces.

 Calm, Pleasant

 Happy, Hopeful

 Laughing

 Relieved

 Serious, Earnest

 Smug, Boastful, Condescending

 Shy, Innocent

 Nervous, Worried

 Scared

 Surprised, Shocked

 Screaming, Hysterical

 Malicious, Sneaky

 Disgusted

 Irritated, Complaining

 Sad, Depressed, Sorry

 Puzzled, Unsure, Thinking

 Sarcastic, Skeptical

 Mumbling, Whispering

 Bored, Disinterested

 Slick, Phony

 Sheepish, Embarrassed

 Proud, Haughty

 Crying

 Excited

 Sick, Disoriented, Tired

 Emotionless

 Crazy, Goofy

 Angry

 Pained, Strained

 Hypnotized, Zombielike

The Feeding of the Five

Scripture for Study:
John 6:5-15

The Scene: A hillside in the country

The Simple Setup: No set is needed. The **Disciple** should stay offstage, out of sight, calling out his or her lines.

Other Options: Add props if you want to (picnic basket, five rolls, two smoked fish) but pretending to have these items is fine. If you have a large group and would like to involve everyone, have other group members play the part of the multitude, sitting on the floor and listening to the far-off, unseen Master.

The Characters:

Person One, the young person in charge of this youth group outing
Person Two, a young athlete
Person Three, a student with a very healthy appetite
Person Four, another hungry teenager
Person Five, still another hungry you-know-what
Disciple, an adult follower of the Master

(*Persons One* through *Five* enter. *Person One* carries or pretends to carry a picnic basket.)

One: I know this GREAT place for a YOUTH GROUP PICNIC. The BEST SPOT on the SEA OF GALILEE. Right over this hill, and . . .

Two: HEY! Look at this CROWD! You said this would be a PRIVATE place.

Three: There must be FIVE THOUSAND men here, not counting women and children!

Four: Some guy is making a SPEECH over there. Something about MUS-TARD SEEDS.

Five: This is RIDICULOUS. Let's go somewhere else.

Two: NO! It took us forever to GET here, and I'm HUNGRY.

One: So are all these OTHER people. I don't like the way they're looking at our PICNIC BASKET.

Disciple: (*Calling from offstage*) EXCUSE me, everybody! The MASTER was wondering whether anybody has any FOOD we could borrow!

Three: BORROW? I'm SURE! Like we'd get it BACK!

Four: I'm STARVING. What's in the basket?

One: Let me see. FIVE SMALL LOAVES and TWO FISH.

Five: WHAT? That's just ONE LOAF apiece, plus TWO-FIFTHS OF A FISH!

Two: Who PACKED this lunch, anyway?

One: My mom. She NEVER packs enough.

Disciple: (*From offstage*) HELLO! Any FOOD out there? We've got a VERY HUNGRY MULTITUDE here!

Three: Looks like WE'RE the only ones with any FOOD.

Four: Well, that's not OUR problem. These people should have stopped at the HIKE-THROUGH window of BURGER KINGDOM on the way OUT here.

Five: WE should have, too. We're going to STARVE.

Two: This is AWFUL. I've got to keep my STRENGTH up for the CAMEL-TOSSING TOURNAMENT next week. COACH says to get THREE SERVINGS FROM THE LOAF GROUP and THREE SERVINGS FROM THE FISH GROUP every single day.

Three: All I had for breakfast was FIGS. I HATE figs.

Disciple: (*Offstage*) Uh, sorry to BOTHER you folks again, but we're STILL looking for a little FOOD. All we need is a LITTLE.

One: What is that guy TALKING about? You can't feed over FIVE THOU-SAND people with only a LITTLE food.

Four: You can't even feed FIVE.

Three: ENOUGH TALKING! The BREAD'S getting stale, and the FISH are starting to smell. Let's EAT!

(They **all** divide up the food.)

Five: HEY, you got THREE-FIFTHS of a FISH!

Two: I did NOT. FINS don't COUNT.

One: Should we ask the BLESSING?

Four: For THIS? It's too SMALL to pray over.

Three: Good. CHOW TIME!

(They **all** eat their shares in two bites.)

All Kids: I'm still HUNGRY!

One: This is the WORST PICNIC EVER.

Three: Well, it's YOUR fault! You should have told your mom there were FIVE of us, not ONE. What were we supposed to DO with the food, MULTIPLY it?

Disciple: (Offstage) ATTENTION! LAST CALL! The MASTER is looking for JUST A BIT OF FOOD; ANYTHING will do. Even A FEW LOAVES AND A COUPLE OF FISH. Anybody?

Five: What is WITH that guy?

Two: Some youth group party THIS turned out to be.

Three: Let's GO.

Four: And let's stop at BURGER KINGDOM on the way back. Or McDAVID'S.

One: FINE!

Disciple: (*Offstage*) SORRY, folks. The Master wanted to provide food for EVERYONE, but no one VOLUNTEERED any. I guess you'll all have to go HOME. I hope you'll come back LATER to hear more of the Master's TEACHING.

Two: Come BACK? Oh, SURE, buddy.

Four: Now THAT would take...

One: A MIRACLE!

For Post-Play Pondering:

1. What concerns kept the five kids from sharing their food? What concerns keep some people from sharing what they have with others?

2. What might have happened if the kids had shared their food? Have you ever let God use some of your time, money, or talent and gotten something out of the experience? What happened?

3. How is our group like these five kids? What needs around us might we be overlooking? What resources do we have that God might be able to do something with?

4. What's the worst thing that could happen if you were to let God use each of the following: (a) your whole day next Saturday, (b) the next $50 you earn, and (c) the most expensive thing you own? What's the best that could happen?

5. What "miracle" that would help other people would you most like to see during the next year? Is there anything you can do to help make it happen? Why or why not?

Other Scriptures for Study:

Exodus 16; 2 Kings 4:1-7; Matthew 25:14-46; Luke 11:29-30.

Leap of Faith

Topic: Sharing Your Beliefs

Scripture for Study:
Colossians 4:5-6

The Scene: A platform from which bungee jumpers jump

The Simple Setup: Set one chair on a platform—or any surface just high enough that the **Jumper** can jump off the back and lie hidden from the audience at the end of the skit. Be sure the floor on which the **Jumper** lands is padded with pillows or a foam-rubber mat. Be ready (or have a group member ready) to make a crashing sound offstage (by dropping a large cardboard carton full of pots and pans, for instance) at the end of the **Jumper's** leap.

Other Options: The **Expert** could read a real magazine or simply pretend to read one. If you want to get fancy, he or she could wear a T-shirt or jacket emblazoned with the words "Acme Bungee Jumpers."

The Characters:

  Expert, a very calm employee of Acme Bungee Jumpers
  Jumper, a nervous, would-be bungee jumper

(The **Expert** lounges in a chair, reading a magazine.)

Expert: NEXT!

(The **Jumper** enters, steps nervously onto the platform, and looks down over the edge.)

Jumper: OH...it certainly is a long way DOWN. (To **Expert**) EXCUSE me...

Expert: Yes?

Jumper: I've come to make the BIG LEAP.

Expert: The BIG LEAP?

Jumper: The big leap into the UNKNOWN.

Expert: The UNKNOWN?

Jumper: Yes. This IS the BUNGEE-JUMPING PLACE, isn't it?

Expert: Why, of COURSE.

Jumper: And you WORK here, right?

Expert: Oh, YES.

Jumper: Well, I want to make a JUMP.

Expert: FINE. Go right AHEAD.

Jumper: Go right AHEAD? But I'm not READY! How do I PREPARE myself? What must I do to be SAFE?

Expert: SAFE? What do you need to be SAFE from?

Jumper: From going down to . . . YOU know. The BAD place. The BOTTOM. I've always heard that if you're NOT PREPARED for the big JUMP, you'll find yourself in a TERRIBLE SPOT.

Expert: SOME believe that. Others DON'T.

Jumper: But what do YOU believe?

Expert: Oh, MY. I couldn't share THAT. It would be too PERSONAL.

Jumper: From going down to. But I want to KNOW! I want to know what will HAPPEN after I JUMP!

Expert: Some believe LIFE AFTER LEAPING is HAPPY and BLISSFUL. OTHERS think that after the jump there is NOTHING—that a person simply CEASES TO EXIST.

Jumper: Well, I don't want to stop existing. I want to be PREPARED.

Expert: 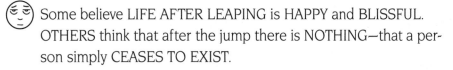 If that's what you WANT.

Jumper: It IS! Now, aren't I supposed to HOOK MYSELF UP to a CORD or something?

Expert: SOME do, some DON'T.

Jumper: Well, as of this minute, I DO! How do I ATTACH it?

Expert: Any way you LIKE. Some believe it looks nice TIED AROUND THEIR NECKS. OTHERS prefer to HOLD IT IN THEIR TEETH. I even saw ONE lady TIE IT TO HER EAR LOBE.

Jumper: But isn't there some kind of ANCHOR that HOLDS the cord? I want to make sure my ANCHOR HOLDS.

Expert: Of COURSE—if you NEED that sort of thing.

Jumper: DON'T I?

Expert: Who am I to say?

Jumper: HEY, what kind of expert ARE you? Have you ever MADE the leap into the unknown?

Expert: My goodness, NO. I'm ALIVE, aren't I?

Jumper: Do you even KNOW anybody who's made the big leap?

Expert: Hmm. No, I don't think I DO.

Jumper: I'm OUTTA here. I'm going to find somebody who knows what he's TALKING about. Somebody who's MADE the great leap or who knows somebody who DID and LIVED TO TELL about it.

Expert: Have it YOUR way.

Jumper: I want to be READY when my time comes.

Expert: That's up to YOU.

Jumper: Nothing PERSONAL, but I think you should find a DIFFERENT LINE OF WORK.

Expert: (Standing up) NO HARD FEELINGS. I wish you WELL.

(The **Expert** pats the off-balance **Jumper** on the back, sending him or her off the rear of the platform and out of sight.)

Jumper: (Screaming as he or she "falls" to the ground) AAAUUUGGGHHH!

(A crash is heard. The **Expert** gazes down over the back edge of the platform, sighs, and speaks after a pause.)

Expert: SHARE my BELIEFS about the BIG LEAP? I could NEVER do THAT. After all, I'd HATE to be one of those people who is so...PUSHY.

(The **Expert** sits down again and takes up the magazine.)

Expert: NEXT!

For Post-Play Pondering:

1. How is facing death like facing a bungee jump? How is it different?

2. Why didn't the Expert want to share his or her beliefs? On a scale of 1 to 10 (with 10 being the hardest), how tough is it for you to share your beliefs about how to prepare for life after death? Why?

3. What did the Jumper want to know? Do most kids you know want to hear about preparing for the next life? Why or why not?

4. What were the results of the Expert's unwillingness to give advice? How is this like— and unlike—what happens when we don't share our faith?

5. When is a person most likely to want to hear about becoming a Christian? Do you know anyone in situations like those? What could you do for a person like that?

Other Scriptures for Study:

Proverbs 14: 5, 7, 12, 15, 25, 27; John 14:1-6; Romans 8:35-39; Hebrews 6:19-20; 1 Peter 3:15-16.

The Simpletons

Topic: Bible Reading

Scripture for Study:
2 Timothy 2:15; 3:14-17

The Scene: The living room of the Simpleton family

The Simple Setup: This is a parody of the TV show *The Simpsons*. Set four chairs in a row to represent a sofa. The **Delivery Person** can use either side of the performance area as the entrance to the Simpleton home. Have someone ready to say, "Ding dong" when the **Delivery Person** rings the imaginary doorbell.

Other Options: The gift-wrapped Bible may be real or imaginary, although a real one will help focus the group's attention. A pacifier in the mouth of **Maggie** will help to identify her. Extra fun could be added by playing a recording of the theme song from *The Simpsons* at the beginning of the skit and having family members assemble on the "sofa" as they do at the start of the TV show.

The Characters:
Delivery Person
Homer Simpleton, the bone-headed father
Marge Simpleton, the blue-haired and befuddled mom
Bart Simpleton, the bratty son
Lisa Simpleton, the brilliant daughter
Maggie Simpleton, the baby who constantly sucks on a pacifier

(The **Simpletons** *are sitting on their living room sofa—except for baby* **Maggie**, *who sits on the floor. The* **Delivery Person**, *carrying a package, walks up to the door and rings the doorbell.* **Marge** *opens the door.*)

Person: Is this the SIMPLETON residence?

Marge: Yes . . .

Person: SPECIAL DELIVERY for HOMER, MARGE, BART, LISA, and MAGGIE SIMPLETON.

Marge: Oh, THANK you. (*Takes the package as the* **Delivery Person** *exits.*) Oh, LOOK! It's GIFT-WRAPPED! I wonder what it could BE?

Homer: Mmm. FOOD! I hope it's FOOD.

Bart: A SKATEBOARD. A skateboard with KNIVES that will pop out the front and LASERS that pierce people's EYEBALLS!

Marge: BART! That's DISGUSTING!

Lisa: No one has yet asked the most IMPORTANT question. Who is it FROM?

Marge: (*Examining the package*) I don't KNOW, Lisa. It doesn't SAY.

Homer: Well, there's only ONE WAY to find OUT. (*Pauses.*) EAT it.

Lisa: You mean OPEN it.

Marge: Oh, THAT'S a good idea. (*She begins to open the package.*) You're so SMART, Lisa. (*She finishes opening the package and holds up a large Bible.*) Oh, LOOK! It's a . . . RECTANGULAR object!

Homer: OOH. Just like a CANDY BAR.

Bart: No, just like a BRIEFCASE full of PLASTIC EXPLOSIVES that could blow up an entire city BLOCK, leaving DESTRUCTION for MILES around!

Marge: BART! That's DISGUSTING!

Lisa: LOOK! There are some LETTERS on the front.

Marge: (*Spelling slowly*) B-I-B-L-E.

Homer: Does that spell CHOCOLATE?

Lisa: No, it spells BIBLE.

Homer: OOH, a BIBLE. (*Pauses.*) What's a BIBLE?

Lisa: WEBSTER defines it as the SACRED SCRIPTURES comprising the OLD and NEW TESTAMENTS.

Homer: OOH. (*Pauses.*) Who's WEBSTER? Wasn't he a little guy on TV?

Marge: Homer, I think Lisa is telling us that this is a SPECIAL kind of BOOK.

Homer: Oh. Does that mean I can put EXTRA CHEESE on it?

Lisa: Daddy, the Bible is not something you EAT. It's something you . . . well, actually, I don't know WHAT you're supposed to do with it.

Bart: Maybe we could take it to the top of the EMPIRE STATE BUILDING and drop it on somebody's HEAD and squish his BRAINS on the SIDEWALK.

Marge: BART! That's DISGUSTING!

Homer: Mmm, SQUISHING. That reminds me of PUDDING. Lots of PUD-DING.

Marge: Maybe I could use it to press AUTUMN LEAVES in. It's good and HEAVY.

Lisa: MOM! You can't use SACRED SCRIPTURES to press LEAVES in!

Marge: Oh. How about using it to prop up that wobbly LEG on the TABLE?

Lisa: THAT would be OK.

Marge: (*Putting the Bible on the floor and setting an imaginary table on it*) THERE. Doesn't THAT look nice?

(*Suddenly baby* **Maggie**, *still sucking on her pacifier, crawls over to the Bible, opens it, and holds it as if she's reading.*)

Lisa: LOOK! Maggie found something to DO with the Bible! She's pre-tending to READ it!

Marge: Isn't that CUTE? PRETENDING to READ the BIBLE!

Homer: Marge, I think we've all learned a valuable LESSON from Maggie.

Marge:		What's THAT, Homer?
Homer:		We should ALL pretend to read the Bible!
Marge:		What a good idea! I'll do it right after I clean the CLOSETS. (*Exits.*)
Lisa:		And I'LL do it right after I do my HOMEWORK. (*Exits.*)
Bart:		And I'LL do it right after I SPRAY PAINT the DOG, put SCORPIONS in Lisa's BED, and set the neighbor's HOUSE on fire. (*Exits.*)
Homer:		And I'LL do it after I EAT EVERYTHING IN THE REFRIGERATOR AND THE CUPBOARDS. (*Pats* **Maggie** *on the head.*) GOOD GIRL, Maggie. Now we can pretend to read the Bible EVERY DAY, thanks to YOU. We have heard the TRUTH out of the mouths of BABES. Well, not exactly out of their MOUTHS. More like out of their HANDS. Or their EYES. Or—oh, NEVER MIND. (*Exits.*)

(**Maggie** *pauses, rolls her eyes, and crawls out, still reading.*)

For Post-Play Pondering:

1. When it comes to the Bible, do you think most people know more than, less than, or about the same amount as the Simpletons? Why?

2. Which of these characters came closest to acting out your attitude toward the Bible? Why?

3. How do some people "pretend" to read the Bible? Why might they do that?

4. If you had to convince each of these characters to *really* read the Bible, how might you go about it?

5. Who do you think might have sent the Simpletons a Bible? Why? Do you think of the Bible as having been "sent" to you? Why or why not?

Other Scriptures for Study:

Psalm 119; James 1:22-25.

Indiana James and the Temple of God

Topic: The Body as God's Temple

Scripture for Study:
1 Corinthians 6:19-20

The Scene: Deep inside a long-neglected temple

The Simple Setup: This is a parody of the movie *Raiders of the Lost Ark*. No set is needed. All the action could take place at the front of your meeting place or the actors
could slowly work their way up a wide center aisle.

Other Options: The following costume additions could enhance the effect: for
Indiana, a leather jacket and fedora hat; for **Hilary**, a formal dress; for **Short**, a
baseball cap; for the **Major**, tan clothing, dark gloves, and boots. The **Major**
could also brandish a toy pistol. For extra fun, try playing (or having group members hum) part of the *Raiders of the Lost Ark* movie theme before and after the skit.

The Characters:
Indiana James, a bullwhip-toting archaeology professor and adventurer
Hilary Diamond, a spoiled and irritating young heiress
Short Tall, 10-year-old street kid and friend of **Indiana**
Major Neglect, a longtime Nazi foe of **Indiana**

▲ ▲ ▲ ▲ ▲ ▲ ▲ ▲

(**Indiana**, **Hilary**, and **Short** enter slowly, single file, as if finding their way through a dim tunnel.)

Hilary: Get me OUT of here, INDIANA JAMES! I don't care whether you ARE
the world's most famous archaeology professor who carries a bull-
whip. You're dealing with HILARY DIAMOND, wealthy HEIRESS!

Indiana: AIRHEAD, you mean.

Hilary: WHAT did you say?

Indiana: I said, "WATCH your HEAD." The ceiling is pretty LOW in this
UNDERGROUND PASSAGEWAY. (*Pauses.*) So THIS is the TEMPLE OF
GOD. Doesn't LOOK like the kind of temple he'd want to LIVE in,
though. It's in pretty bad SHAPE.

Short:  Dr. JAMES! Dr. JAMES!

Indiana: What IS it, SHORT FAT?

Short: That's Short TALL. A DOOR is closing behind us! And the TUNNEL is filling up with POISONOUS GAS!

(They **all** cough.)

Indiana: It's SMOKE! The CARETAKER of this temple must be a SMOKER. Doesn't he realize the DAMAGE he's doing to the temple? I HATE smoke.

Hilary: I can't BREATHE!

Indiana: Try to CONSERVE OXYGEN— 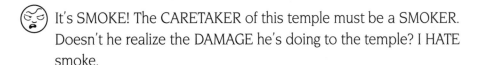 by CLOSING your MOUTH!

Short: Dr. JAMES! There's a SECRET PANEL in the wall. Maybe if I PUSH it ... There! The smoke is blowing AWAY!

Indiana: Good WORK, Tall Round.

Short: That's SHORT... NEVER MIND.

Hilary: What's that SPLASHING sound?

Indiana: We're in a STREAM now. The BLOODSTREAM. Let's FOLLOW it.

Hilary: But my FEET—they're getting NUMB!

Indiana: There's a powerful TOXIN in the bloodstream. (He *sniffs*.) ALCO-HOL—and OTHER DRUGS. The caretaker is abusing the temple with DRUGS. I HATE that!

Hilary: Now my LEGS are numb! I can't WALK!

Indiana: SQUARE ROUND! YOU take ONE arm; I'LL take the OTHER!

(They **all** begin to shake as if the floor is moving.)

Hilary: What's that SHAKING? It feels like an EARTHQUAKE!

Indiana: The PILLARS of the TEMPLE are starting to COLLAPSE! The caretaker doesn't get enough SLEEP, and MENTAL FATIGUE sets in. RUN for it!

(They **all** run in place.)

Short: Dr. JAMES! Dr. JAMES! The FLOOR is giving way!

Indiana: It's WEAK—built entirely of JUNK FOOD! Watch your step!

(The **Major** enters and takes a place at one side of the stage.)

Short: Dr. JAMES! We're almost OUT! But who's that man in the uniform, standing by the door and pointing the GUN at us?

Indiana: (*Stopping, as do the others, and addressing the* **Major**) MAJOR NEGLECT!

Major: (*With a German accent*) SO, Dr. James. We meet AGAIN. How do you like what the caretaker and I have DONE to this temple? Quite a SIGHT, wouldn't you say?

Indiana: It's a SIGHT, all right. You've RUINED a PRICELESS DWELLING PLACE that doesn't BELONG to you.

Major: And now, you and your friends are going to be part of its FALL. FAREWELL, Dr. James. (*Points the gun at* **Indiana**.)

Hilary: NO YOU DON'T! (*She rushes the* **Major** *and knocks him out with a faked punch.*) NOBODY'S going to trap ME here. I have a DINNER PARTY to go to!

Short: Dr. JAMES! The temple is COLLAPSING!

Indiana: The door to the brain has rusted SHUT! It hasn't been USED in YEARS.

Hilary: THAT'S obvious!

Indiana: We'll have to push TOGETHER. Ready, set, NOW!

(They **all** push through.)

Hilary: We MADE it!

Indiana: I wish we could say the same for the TEMPLE. It's a SHAMBLES.

Hilary: How could the caretaker treat such a BEAUTIFUL TEMPLE that way?

Indiana: I don't know. Maybe he forgot who LIVED in it.

Short: Where do you think God will live NOW, Dr. James?

Indiana: I don't know, son. He used to like dwelling in the tabernacle, enthroned in the ARK OF THE COVENANT. Too bad it's LOST.

Short: The LOST ARK? Maybe we should try to FIND it.

(**All** three look at each other, then shake their heads.)

All: NAAH! (Exit.)

For Post-Play Pondering:

1. What is a temple for? What do people do there?

2. How would people react if gangs sprayed graffiti on the churches, synagogues, mosques, or shrines in our town? on the gravestones in cemeteries? Why?

3. What do the temple and the caretaker stand for in this skit? Who owns the temple? Why?

4. Can you think of any other ways in which people abuse the "temple"? What's your answer to Hilary's question about how the caretaker could treat such a beautiful temple that way?

5. If God is willing to turn our bodies into his temples, what does that tell us about him? about the relationship God wants with us? about our bodies?

▶Other Scriptures for Study:

John 14:23-25; Romans 6:11-14; 12:1-2; 1 Timothy 4:7-8; 1 Peter 4:1-7.

The Bomb Squad

Topic: Missions

Scripture for Study:
Matthew 28:19-20

The Scene: Headquarters of the Police Department Bomb Squad

The Simple Setup: You'll need two chairs for the actors to sit on. A small table with a telephone on it would be a good idea, though the actors could pantomime answering the phone if necessary. In either case, include the following sound effects: a telephone ringing (an actual phone or just someone saying, "Ring, ring") and explosions (a recording or someone making the appropriate noises into an offstage microphone). The doughnuts may be real or imagined.

Other Options: The actors could wear police-type uniforms or protective bomb-squad gear (goggles or motorcycle helmets, heavy gloves, chest pads or aprons, or other protective clothing).

The Characters:
   Officer One, an unenergetic member of the Police Department Bomb Squad
   Officer Two, a similar member of the same squad

(The phone rings. **Officer One** *answers it.)*

One: POLICE DEPARTMENT BOMB SQUAD. How can I HELP you? *(Pauses.)* You've found a BOMB in your house? It's about to go OFF? Where do you LIVE? Twenty MILES from here? That's not even in our town. Thank goodness WE'LL be safe! Well, good LUCK! *(Hangs up.)*

(Sound: Explosion in the distance.)

Two: What did they call US for? WE don't live there.

One: YEAH. They ought to have their OWN bomb squad.

Two: RIGHT. Do they expect us to pack up and go to some STRANGE PLACE we've never BEEN before, just because they're in terrible DANGER?

One: They're so far away, we probably don't even speak their LANGUAGE.

Two: I bet they eat WEIRD FOOD, too. 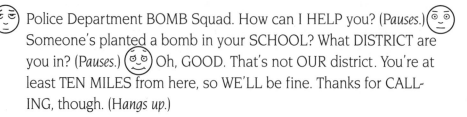 Pass the DOUGHNUTS, will you?

*(They munch on doughnuts. The phone rings. **One** answers it.)*

One: Police Department BOMB Squad. How can I HELP you? *(Pauses.)* Someone's planted a bomb in your SCHOOL? What DISTRICT are you in? *(Pauses.)* Oh, GOOD. That's not OUR district. You're at least TEN MILES from here, so WE'LL be fine. Thanks for CALL- ING, though. *(Hangs up.)*

(Sound: Explosion in the distance, a bit louder than the first.)

Two: They didn't really WANT us to come.

One: NAH. They probably have their OWN way of dealing with explosives.

Two: They didn't really WANT us to come. YEP. They wouldn't want us to BARGE IN and INTERFERE. Want another DOUGHNUT?

*(They munch on doughnuts. The phone rings. **One** answers it.)*

One: Police Department BOMB Squad. How can I HELP you? *(Pauses.)* TERRORISTS have put a bomb in your SKYSCRAPER? What's your ADDRESS? *(Pauses.)* Well, THAT'S a relief. You're not in OUR neighborhood. Have a nice DAY. *(Hangs up.)*

(Sound: Explosion in the distance, louder than the previous one.)

Two: Where was THAT one from?

One: A pretty NASTY part of town. Lots of VIOLENCE. A real JUNGLE.

Two: Why would we want to go to a place like THAT? They probably don't even have DOUGHNUTS.

*(They munch on doughnuts. The phone rings. **One** answers it.)*

One: Police Department BOMB Squad. How can I— WHAT? This is the HOSPITAL? YOU have a bomb, TOO? But you're just a few BLOCKS from here! Is it a BIG bomb or a LITTLE bomb? (*Pauses.*) Just enough to blow up your BUILDING? GREAT! Then we can stay right here. (*Pauses.*) HUH? Oh, I don't know—try unhooking some of the WIRES from those DOOHICKEY things. YOU'LL figure it out. (*Hangs up.*)

(*Sound: Loud explosion from offstage.*)

Two: The HOSPITAL?

One: Yeah. Hospitals give me the CREEPS. They have DISEASES and stuff. If we went THERE, we might get SICK!

Two: RIGHT. Then we couldn't eat any more DOUGHNUTS.

(*They munch on doughnuts. The phone rings.* **One** *answers it.*)

One: Police Department BOMB Squad. How can I HELP you? (*Pauses.*) Oh, HI, CHIEF. How are YOU? (*Pauses.*) Well, now, hold ON, sir. (*Pauses.*) Yes, sir, I REMEMBER what you told us. You said, "GO into all the WORLD and DEFUSE the EXPLOSIVES." (*Pauses.*) But, SIR, we…uh…thought you were KIDDING. (*Pauses.*) NO, sir, you DON'T sound like you're kidding. (*Pauses.*) YES, sir. Right AWAY, sir. (*Hangs up.*)

Two: UH-oh.

One: The CHIEF says we have to get OFF our rear ENDS and go wherever the BOMBS are. Or…

Two: Or WHAT?

One: Or we'll have to stop calling ourselves the BOMB squad.

Two: Well, there's only ONE thing we can do.

One: I KNOW. The RIGHT thing.

Two: YEP. No matter how HARD it is.

One: No matter how much SACRIFICE it takes.

Two: Let's DO it!

(*The phone rings.* **One** *answers it.*)

One: Hello. Police Department DOUGHNUT Squad. How can I HELP you?

(*They exit, munching doughnuts and* **One** *carrying the phone.*)

For Post-Play Pondering:

1. Would "Safety First" be a good motto for a bomb squad? for a Christian? Why or why not?

2. What reasons did the officers give for not following up on the calls? How are they like the reasons people give for not being involved in missions?

3. Is every follower of Jesus to be a member of the spiritual "bomb squad"? Why or why not?

4. How close does someone have to be to you before you care whether or not that person chooses to follow Christ? Do you think it's easier to tell a friend or a stranger about Jesus? Why?

5. If Jesus called our group with a message about missions, what do you think he might say?

Other Scriptures for Study:

The book of Jonah; Luke 10:25-37; Philippians 1:12-30; Jude 22-23.

Godbusters

The Scene: The Smith home

The Simple Setup: This is a parody of the movie *Ghostbusters*. No setup is needed.
Bunk and **Fraudman** can use either side of the performance area as the entrance
to the Smith home. Have someone make a knocking sound when **Bunk** knocks on
the invisible door.

Other Options: Bunk and **Fraudman** could simply pantomime their props (the scientific devices and the piece of paper), but using actual props would enhance the
effect. For the scientific devices, try using hand-held video games or TV remote
controls.

The Characters:
   Ms. Smith, an excited young woman
   Dr. Bunk, a no-nonsense investigator of supernatural phenomena
   Professor Fraudman, the doctor's absent-minded assistant

(**Ms. Smith** *is pacing back and forth.* **Bunk** *and* **Fraudman** *walk up to an imaginary door at one side*
of the stage; **Bunk** *knocks and* **Smith** *opens the door.*)

Smith: Oh, thank goodness you're HERE! You must be from the
INSTITUTE for SUPERNATURAL STUDIES.

Bunk: That's RIGHT. I'm DR. BUNK, and this is PROFESSOR FRAUDMAN.

Smith: I'm Ms. Smith. Come right IN.

(**Bunk** *and* **Fraudman** *come in and look around using scientific-looking equipment.*)

Bunk: Any unusual READINGS, Professor?

Fraudman: Nothing YET, Doctor.

Bunk: Perhaps that's because you're using a Nintendo GAME BOY,
Professor. Try the ECTOPLASMIC MAGNETROMETER instead.

Fraudman: Oh. Yes. Sorry. (*He uses a different piece of equipment.*)

Bunk: As you know, Ms. Smith, the Institute for Supernatural Studies investigates the UNEXPLAINED, the PARANORMAL, and the SUPERNATURAL.

Smith: Oh, YES! That's why I called. I KNEW you'd want to investigate.

Bunk: Very well. Have you been experiencing … GHOSTS? Evil SPIRITS? UFOS? BIGFOOT?

Smith: No.

Fraudman: CHILLS? THRILLS? Yellow, waxy BUILDUP?

Bunk: (*To **Fraudman***) WHAT?

Fraudman: I just THREW that one IN. Sorry.

Bunk: Ms. Smith, we're VERY busy. Exactly WHAT kind of supernatural phenomena have you experienced?

Smith: GOD.

Bunk: What?

Smith: GOD. You know, the Supreme BEING.

Bunk: I've HEARD the name—I think. Professor, reset your sensors to GOD.

Fraudman: I … don't have a GOD setting. I have one for UNICORNS, though.

Bunk: That's good enough. (**Fraudman** *points the device around the room.*)

Smith: See, I've been noticing evidence that GOD is involved in my LIFE. LITTLE things. Things I'd IGNORED before. Like this WALL, for instance.

Bunk: (*Pointing a device at the wall*) AH! NOW we're getting somewhere! What have you SEEN on the wall? Slime? Blood? Flies?

Fraudman: A glowing image in the shape of MADONNA?

Bunk: I think you mean THE Madonna, Professor.

Fraudman: Oh. Sorry.

Smith: No, I mean the wall ITSELF. If God didn't provide my RENT money, I wouldn't have that wall's PROTECTION against the wind and rain. And if God hadn't given people the ability to cut boards, NONE of us would have walls.

Bunk: (*After a pause*) That's IT?

Smith: Oh, there's MUCH more! The other day God pointed me to a BIBLE verse that reminded me that I can do ALL THINGS THROUGH HIM. At the mall, I saw this cute little boy and kept thinking what a great ARTIST God is when he DESIGNS people. And just this MORNING, when I was TALKING to God . . .

Bunk: Just a minute. You TALK to God?

Smith: Why, YES. It's called PRAYING.

Bunk: I think we've heard ENOUGH, Ms. Smith. We investigate the INCREDIBLE, not the IMPOSSIBLE.

Smith: But . . .

Bunk: Professor, are you getting any READINGS?

Fraudman: (*Consulting the device*) No . . . but if you ever want to put another BATHROOM in, miss, there's a WATER PIPE right about HERE. (*Points to the wall.*)

Bunk: PROFESSOR!

Fraudman: Sorry.

Bunk: Let's GO, Professor.

Fraudman: Yes, LET'S.

Bunk: Ms. Smith, call us if you find any real evidence of supernatural activity. Like MOANING, CLANKING CHAINS, OR POOR TV RECEPTION. Until then, do NOT bother us again. We're MUCH too busy looking into IMPORTANT cases. Good DAY.

Fraudman: (To **Smith**) Sorry.

(**Bunk** and **Fraudman** exit the house and come to the front of the stage.)

Bunk: PATHETIC! Some people will believe ANYTHING. What's our NEXT case?

Fraudman: (Consulting a piece of paper) A child on Maple Street is reporting that every time he LOSES A TOOTH, a QUARTER mysteriously appears under his PILLOW.

Bunk: Why, it's that TOOTH FAIRY again! He's a CLEVER one, but he can't escape me FOREVER! We'll catch him THIS time! Bring the EQUIP-MENT! (Exits.)

Fraudman: Whatever you SAY, Doc! (Shrugs at the audience and exits.)

For Post-Play Pondering:

1. When people talk about the supernatural, do you feel bothered, bored, interested, or amused? Why?

2. Do you think more people want to *know* God or know *about* God? Explain.

3. Which of the following do you think belong in the category of "unsolved mysteries": what happens to people after they die, whether ESP works, whether God exists, whether it's possible to communicate with God, and how the universe came into being? Why?

4. If God decided to perform miracles to prove he exists, how often do you think he'd have to do them to keep people convinced? What "proof" of God's existence do you think would be most convincing to the people you know?

5. What evidence do you have that God has been involved in your life during the past six months? If you can't think of any, how do you feel about that?

Other Scriptures for Study:

1 Kings 19:1-13; Psalm 14; Luke 11:29-32; Philippians 4:13.

The "Bad" Samaritan

Topic: Racism

Scripture for Study:
Luke 10:25-37

The Scene: A remote road in New Testament times

The Simple Setup: No set is needed. The entrance should be a door or screen from which the **Traveler**, **Priest**, and **Levite** may stumble as if they've been thrown. The **Narrator** should be offstage.

Other Options: The skit's impact might be heightened if the **Samaritan** is played by a person whose race is not well represented in your group—as long as that person doesn't mind being singled out. As for costumes, try a robe for the **Samaritan**; long underwear for the **Traveler**, **Priest**, and **Levite**; and a blue shirt and pants for the **Police Officer**.

The Characters:
Narrator
Samaritan
Traveler
Priest
Levite
Police Officer

Narrator: (*From offstage*) A MAN was going down from JERUSALEM to JERICHO when he fell into the hands of ROBBERS.

(The **Traveler** stumbles in as if thrown; he falls on the floor, stage right, as if unconscious.)

Narrator: (*From offstage*) They STRIPPED him of his CLOTHES, BEAT him, and went AWAY—leaving him HALF DEAD. (*Pauses.*) A SAMARITAN was going down the SAME road.

(The **Samaritan** wanders in; he discovers the **Traveler** and kneels down to help him or her.)

Narrator: (*From offstage*) And when he saw the TRAVELER, the SAMARITAN took PITY on him. He went to the man and began to BANDAGE his WOUNDS, pouring on OIL and WINE. But then the Traveler woke UP.

Traveler: What HAPPENED? (*Looks at* **Samaritan**.) HEY! You're a—a SAMARITAN! You HALF-BREED! Get your HANDS off me!

Samaritan: But I'm only trying to HELP. You were lying here UNCONSCIOUS and...

Traveler: YUCK! Don't TOUCH me! And what's that WINE smell? You're DRUNK!

Samaritan: NO, no! I was putting OIL and WINE on your WOUNDS to help them HEAL.

Traveler: YEAH, I BET! I know all ABOUT you people. DRUNK all the time. Can't hold a JOB. You're all on WELFARE. And you LOOK funny, too.

Samaritan: If you don't get help with these INJURIES, you'll be in pretty bad SHAPE.

Traveler: DON'T tell me what to do, you—you—SAMARITAN! Leave me ALONE! (**Traveler** *faints*.)

Samaritan: (*Sighing and walking away*) ALL RIGHT. If that's the way you WANT it.

(*The* **Samaritan** *walks in place, facing the audience*.)

Narrator: (*From offstage*) A PRIEST also was going down from Jerusalem to Jericho when HE, TOO, fell into the hands of robbers.

(*The* **Priest** *stumbles in as if thrown; he falls on the floor, center stage, as if unconscious*.)

Narrator: (*From offstage*) They STRIPPED him of his CLOTHES, BEAT him, and went AWAY—leaving HIM half dead. But the SAMARITAN was going down the SAME road.

(*The* **Samaritan** *turns and discovers the* **Priest**.)

Samaritan: Not AGAIN! (*The* **Samaritan** *kneels to help the* **Priest**.)

Narrator: And when the Samaritan SAW the Priest, he took PITY on him. He went to the man and began to BANDAGE his WOUNDS. But then the Priest woke UP.

Priest: OW! My LEG! (*Looks at the* **Samaritan**.)OH.That's KIND of you, young man, but it really isn't ... NECESSARY.

Samaritan: Oh, IT'S necessary. You have a broken LEG. Probably broken RIBS, too.

Priest: YES, well ... it's not that I'm UNCOMFORTABLE with SAMARITANS, you understand. No, not at ALL. Some of my BEST FRIENDS are Samaritans. So you can be on your WAY now. You're a CREDIT to your RACE, young man. Not like those LAZY Samaritans. Or the MILITANTS you hear so much about. I'm sure you'll MAKE something of yourself.

Samaritan: Like a DOCTOR, maybe?

Priest: Well, let's not expect TOO much. Perhaps a VETERINARIAN. Now, go ON. Don't worry about ME. I'll be FINE. Just FINE. (*He faints.*)

(*The* **Samaritan** *gets up, shaking his head. He walks in place again, facing the audience.*)

Narrator: (*From offstage*) ANOTHER man, a LEVITE, was going down from Jerusalem to Jericho when HE also fell into the hands of robbers.

(*The* **Levite** *comes stumbling in as if thrown; he falls on the floor, stage left, as if unconscious.*)

Narrator: (*From offstage*) They stripped HIM of his clothes, beat HIM, and went AWAY—leaving HIM half dead. But the SAMARITAN was going down the SAME road.

(*The* **Samaritan** *turns and discovers the* **Levite**.)

Samaritan: MAN, I've got to find a different ROAD! (*He kneels down to help.*)

Narrator: (*From offstage*) And when he SAW the Levite, the Samaritan took PITY on him. He went to the man and began to bandage HIS wounds ...

Levite: OHHH. (*Looks at the* **Samaritan**.) HELP! POLICE! It's a SAMARITAN!

Samaritan: PLEASE, calm DOWN. I'm only trying to BANDAGE your WOUNDS.

Levite: Trying to lift my WALLET, you mean! You Samaritans are all ALIKE! DEADBEATS! CRIMINALS! THIEVES! (*Pauses.*) HELP, POLICE!

(The **Police Officer** enters.)

Officer: (*To **Levite***) What seems to be the TROUBLE, sir?

Levite: This SAMARITAN! He STRIPPED me of my CLOTHES, BEAT me, and left me HALF DEAD. And now he's trying to ROB me!

Samaritan: There's been a MISTAKE. I was only trying to HELP!

Officer: (*To **Samaritan***) RIGHT, pal. I know YOUR kind. No doubt you're the one who's been robbing ALL the travelers on this road. You can't walk TEN FEET without running into another BODY. You're under ARREST. You have the right to remain SILENT...

(The **Officer** leads him away.)

Levite: Throw the BOOK at him! The only GOOD Samaritan... is a DEAD Samaritan! (*He faints.*)

Narrator: (*From offstage, after a pause*) WHICH of these do you think was a NEIGHBOR to the Samaritan? (*Pauses.*) I couldn't think of any, EITHER.

For Post-Play Pondering:

1. What does this skit tell you about what *all* Samaritans were like? about *all* travelers, priests, and Levites? What does that tell you about prejudice?

2. Which of the characters do you think was most prejudiced? Why?

3. Which of the following do you think Jesus would do: (a) laugh at a racial joke; (b) advise a young follower not to marry someone of a different race; (c) demonstrate peacefully for the civil rights of minority groups; (d) call someone a racist; or (e) take part in a violent, racially-motivated riot? Why?

4. If you had to be a member of another race for a year, which would you choose? Why?

5. Which of the characters in this skit is our group most like? How do you feel about that? How do you think God feels about that?

6. How do you think God wants you to think, talk, and act toward those of other races? Support your answer from Scripture.

Other Scriptures for Study:

Leviticus 19:15-18; James 2:1-9.

The No-Talk Talk Show

Topic: Prayer

Scripture for Study:
Psalm 32:3-7

The Scene: The set of a late-night TV talk show

The Simple Setup: This is a parody of the *Late Show With David Letterman*. A desk (or card table) and chair are needed for **Laterman**, plus a guest chair beside his desk. **Paul** stands to one side of the stage. The **Announcer**, who stands on the opposite side, needs a large cardboard sign that says, "Applause and Cheering." If possible, provide a drumroll as indicated—either live, on tape, or electronically synthesized.

Other Options: Try putting a keyboard in front of **Paul** and have him improvise theme and transitional music if he can. Costumes such as suits for **Laterman** and **Buddy**, funky clothes for **Paul**, a glamorous dress for **Angela**, and casual clothes for the **Announcer** could be added.

The Characters:

Announcer, smooth-voiced and full of energy
David Laterman, the sarcastic TV talk show host
Paul Shaker, the hip band leader and sidekick
Buddy Millstone, an elderly, has-been actor
Angela Fluff, an empty-headed actress

Announcer: From NEW LIFE—where the STREETS are paved with GOOD INTENTIONS—it's *The* BETTER LATE THAN NEVER SHOW *With* DAVID LATERMAN! Tonight Dave's guests include . . . GOD! And NOW . . . a man who never puts off TOMORROW what he can put off TODAY . . . DAVID LATERMAN!

*(The **Announcer** holds up the "Applause and Cheering" sign. **Laterman** enters and stands center stage.)*

Laterman: Thank you, and welcome to the PROGRAM. Tonight's show is SO GOOD you may actually want to PLUG IN YOUR TELEVISION SET before WATCHING! A VERY SPECIAL GUEST is with us— the SUPREME BEING! We'll be TALKING WITH GOD! But first, let's SAY HELLO TO OUR GOOD FRIEND, Mr. PAUL SHAKER!

*(The **Announcer** holds up the "Applause and Cheering" sign as **Laterman** sits at the desk.)*

Paul: THANK you, Dave. What an EXCITING EVENING—the CREATOR OF THE UNIVERSE on OUR SHOW! Can we talk to him NOW?

Laterman: LATER, Paul, LATER. Right now it's time for our TOP FIVE LIST from the home office in Colorado Springs. Here are . . . the TOP FIVE WAYS TO MISPRONOUNCE "CHRONICLES"! *(Drumroll begins and continues through the reading of the list.)* Number Five . . . BARNA-CLES! Number Four . . . CROP DUSTERS! Number Three . . . POPSICLES! Number Two . . . CHRONIC ILLNESS! And the NUM-BER ONE WAY TO MISPRONOUNCE "CHRONICLES" . . . CORIN-THIANS!

*(The **Announcer** holds up the "Applause and Cheering" sign.)*

Paul: That was TRULY INSPIRING. NOW, it must be time to TALK TO GOD.

Laterman: LATER, Paul, LATER. Our FIRST guest is the star of TV's *This Old Sitcom!* Ladies and gentlemen, please welcome . . . Mr. BUDDY MILLSTONE!

*(The **Announcer** holds up the sign. **Buddy** enters slowly and sits next to **Laterman**.)*

Laterman: Buddy, you're so OLD everybody thought you were DEAD.

Buddy: Well, I'm NOT. *(Clears his throat and just sits.)*

Paul: *(After a pause)* Uh, Dave—is it time to TALK TO GOD yet?

Laterman: LATER, Paul, LATER. *(To **Buddy**)* Well, thanks for being WITH us, Buddy. Come back and see us AGAIN, unless you're DEAD. Mr. BUDDY MILLSTONE, ladies and gentlemen!

*(The **Announcer** holds up the "Applause and Cheering" sign as **Buddy** exits.)*

Paul: Well, THAT was a waste of time. Now we can TALK TO GOD.

Laterman: (face) LATER, Paul, LATER. (face) Ladies and gentlemen, our next guest appears in the upcoming motion picture *A Leech of Their Own*. Please welcome the lovely and talented ANGELA FLUFF!

(*The* **Announcer** *holds up the sign as* **Angela** *enters and sits next to* **Laterman**.)

Angela: (face) SO, Dave—do you like my DRESS?

Laterman: (face) It's STUNNING.

Angela: (face) How about my SHOES?

Laterman: (face) VERY nice.

Angela: (face) (*Pauses.*) Is my HAIR OK?

Laterman: (face) It's FINE! Are we going to talk about your APPEARANCE all NIGHT?

Angela: (face) What ELSE is there?

Laterman: (face) (*Pause*) Well, NOTHING. SORRY. I don't know what came OVER me.

(**Angela** *clears her throat and just sits.*)

Paul: (*After a pause*) Uh, Dave—is it time to TALK TO GOD yet?

Laterman: LATER, Paul, LATER. (*To* **Angela**) Well, Angie, come back and see us NEXT time you get your hair done! (face) Ms. ANGELA FLUFF!

(*The* **Announcer** *holds up the sign as* **Angela** *exits.*)

Paul: And NOW the moment we've all been WAITING for. Let's TALK TO GOD!

Laterman: LATER, Paul, LATER! (face) It's time for a segment we call STUPID HAT TRICKS! A man from our studio audience is going to put his HAT on his HEAD—using only ONE HAND!

Paul: Now, JUST A MINUTE! This has gone FAR ENOUGH! We can't keep the MAKER OF ALL THINGS waiting FOREVER!

Laterman: Of COURSE we can, Paul. He's ETERNAL, remember? With him a day is as ONE THOUSAND YEARS. Or maybe it's the other way AROUND.

Paul: But …

Laterman: OK, Paul. Just for you, we'll SKIP the man with the hat. Ladies and gentlemen, our LAST guest is known AROUND THE GLOBE as the BEGINNING and the END. He's been called ALL-POWERFUL AND ALL-KNOWING. His story is told in the world's MOST POPULAR BOOK, the BIBLE. Please welcome …

Announcer: Uh, Dave? DAVE? (*Pauses.*) I'm afraid we've run out of TIME.

Laterman: Oh. Well, we'll just bring God BACK some OTHER night. We can always talk to him … LATER.

Paul: But …

Laterman: Be with us TOMORROW night, folks, when our guests will be the group SMASHING SQUASHES—and a lady who collects USED EARPLUGS. GOOD NIGHT!

(The **Announcer** *holds up the sign.* **Paul** *exits, shaking his head.*)

Announcer: (*After the applause stops*) SAY, Dave … could YOU go tell God why we didn't have TIME for him? (*Exits.*)

Laterman: Uh … maybe LATER! (*He runs out, looking nervously over his shoulder.*)

For Post-Play Pondering:

1. If you had to explain the talk show host's behavior to God, what would you say?

2. How would "talking with God" on a TV show be different from praying to him? How would it be similar?

3. What "top five" activities would most people rather do than talk to God? Why? Would the list be the same for both Christians and non-Christians? Explain.

4. If you could talk to God only on Tuesdays between 2 and 3 a.m., would you do it? Why or why not?

5. If you prayed just three minutes more each day than you do now, how might your life be different in a year? What if you prayed 10 minutes more each day?

Other Scriptures for Study:

Matthew 14:22-23; 26:36-46; Colossians 4:2-4; 1 Thessalonians 5:16-18.

The Amusement Park

Topic: Christians and Fun

Scripture for Study:
Ecclesiastes 5:18-19

The Scene: An amusement park

The Simple Setup: Three chairs representing the roller coaster seat should be placed side by side, facing the audience, in the center of the performance area. The rest of the action can be pantomimed without props.

Other Options: If you have access to a sound effects tape or CD, you could add calliope music and roller coaster noises in the background.

The Characters:
Chris, an unenthusiastic Christian guy or girl
Pat, another unenthused Christian guy or girl
Sam, still another you-know-what

▲ ▲ ▲ ▲ ▲ ▲ ▲ ▲

Chris: Well, here we ARE. The AMUSEMENT park.

Sam: (*Yawning*) There's the FUN house. Let's go IN.

Chris and Pat: (*Together*) OK.

Pat: The hall of MIRRORS.

(*Facing the audience, **all** make faces at themselves in imaginary mirrors.*)

Chris: Look at US. We look really STUPID.

Sam and Pat: (*Together*) YEAH.

Chris: HEY, you KNOW something?

Pat: What?

Chris:  Did you ever notice that CHRISTIANS never get to have any FUN?

Sam: THAT'S for sure.

Chris: NON-Christians are the only ones who get to have a GOOD TIME.

Pat: Yeah. Let's get SNOW CONES.

Chris and Sam: (Together) OK.

(**All** pantomime buying snow cones, which they lick.)

Chris: Kids at SCHOOL don't have to worry about all those DO'S and DON'TS.

Pat: RIGHT. I HATE it.

Sam: There are the BUMPER CARS. Let's go on THOSE.

Chris and Pat: (Together) OK.

(**All** crouch down and pretend to ride bumper cars as they say their lines.)

Chris: All these RULES drive me CRAZY. Don't get DRUNK. Don't have SEX.

Sam: Don't lie down in the middle of the FREEWAY.

Chris and Pat: (Together) YEAH.

Pat: Let's go have a CORN DOG.

Chris and Sam: (Together) OK.

(**All** get up and pantomime buying corn dogs, which they eat as they talk.)

Pat: Take TANYA at SCHOOL. SHE gets to do all the DRUGS she wants.

Chris: At least she COULD until she went to that HOSPITAL for ADDICTS.

Sam: Yeah. I bet THAT'S a fun place, TOO.

Chris: And CHURCH. That's the WORST.

Pat: ONE boring meeting after ANOTHER, 24 hours a DAY, seven days a WEEK.

Sam: NON-Christians NEVER have to go to church. THEY can do whatever they WANT.

Chris: Let's have some COTTON CANDY, some POP, and some CURLY FRIES.

Sam and Pat: (*Together*) OK.

(**All** *pantomime giving money to a vendor and stuffing their faces.*)

Sam: (*Mouth full*) Being a Christian is a DRAG. You never get a taste of the GOOD things in life.

Chris and Pat: (*Together, mouths full*) Yeah.

Sam: Let's go on the NUCLEAR HURRICANE.

Chris: You mean the TALLEST, FASTEST ROLLER COASTER in NORTH AMERICA?

Sam: Yep.

Chris and Pat: (*Together*) OK.

(**All** *sit on the chairs and pretend to ride a roller coaster bumping up and down as they speak.*)

Pat: Sometimes I wonder whether it's WORTH it to be a Christian.

Chris and Sam: (*Together*) Yeah.

Pat: (*Jolting right, as do the others*) I mean, what do you get OUT of it, anyway?

Chris: (*Jolting left, as do others*) Just eternal LIFE, THAT'S all.

Pat and Sam: (*Together*) Yeah.

Chris: Here comes the BIG one. (**All** *rise in the seat.*) Up ... up ... and ...

All: (*With a long yell, gripping an imaginary safety bar*) AAAUUUGGGHHH!

(*They **all** sway from side to side, then stop abruptly, as if at the bottom of the hill.*)

Chris: OHHH. I don't FEEL so good.

Pat and Sam: (*Together*) Me NEITHER.

(*They **all** get out, staggering.*)

Chris: SEE? Christians NEVER have any fun.

Pat and Sam: (*Together*) YEAH.

Chris: So what do you want to do NEXT Saturday?

Pat: I don't know. We could go to the MALL, or WINDSURFING, or SCUBA DIVING. Or HOT-AIR BALLOONING ... (**All** *exit.*)

For Post-Play Pondering:

1. Do you ever feel like any of these characters felt? Why or why not?

2. Why were these characters having such a lousy time?

3. Do you think it's true that Christians have less fun than non-Christians? Why or why not?

4. If Jesus were invited to an amusement park, do you think he'd go? If so, what might he do there? If not, what might he do instead?

5. If there were no afterlife rewards for Christians, would you still want to be one? Why or why not?

6. What are 10 fun things that Christian kids can do? Which would you like our group to do more of?

Other Scriptures for Study:

Jeremiah 12:1-2; Proverbs 14:30; Psalm 23; Romans 8:18; Philippians 3:1, 7-14.

The Used Teenager Lot

Topic: Relationships

Scripture for Study:
Philippians 2:3-4

The Scene: The lot at Honest Al's Premium Pre-Owned Price-Cutters

The Simple Setup: No set is needed. **Al** should have a handkerchief in his pocket. Instead of explaining beforehand where the action is taking place, let the group discover this as the skit progresses.

Other Options: **Al** could wear a loud, mismatched blazer and pants—or even a cowboy hat with a white or light-colored suit.

The Characters:
    Customer, a high school guy or girl
    Honest Al, a slick salesman
    Person One, a teenage guy or girl
    Person Two, a teenage girl
    Person Three, a teenage guy or girl

▲ ▲ ▲ ▲ ▲ ▲ ▲ ▲

(*Persons One, Two, and Three enter, stand at equal distances apart across the stage, face the audience, and look sadly down at the floor. They remain this way throughout the skit unless otherwise noted. Al enters, full of energy, looking around for customers. Finally the Customer enters and comes up to Al.*)

Customer:		EXCUSE me. Are you HONEST AL?
Al:		That's ME, kid! Welcome to HONEST AL'S PREMIUM PRE-OWNED PRICE-CUTTERS—home of the FIVE THOUSAND-FOOT WARRANTY.
Customer:		GREAT. See, I'm looking for …
Al:		Kid, no matter WHAT you're looking for, we've GOT it. Look AROUND you. Over THREE HUNDRED MODELS to choose from. You won't find another new OR used lot like this in the ENTIRE TRI-STATE AREA.
Customer:		Good, because I really need …

Al: I know EXACTLY what you need, kid. You need something that RUNS. You need something that LOOKS GOOD. You need something CHEAP. Take a look at THIS beauty over here. (*Brings* **Customer** *to stand in front of* **Person One**.) This one's a CLASSIC. Formerly used by a LITTLE OLD SENIOR from PASADENA.

Customer: But ... but this is a ...

Al: I KNOW what it is—the BARGAIN of the CENTURY! That little old senior hardly spent ANY TIME with this one. Kept PROMISING to, but never did. PROMISES were broken, but this little number was barely used at ALL.

Customer: I ... I don't think you UNDERSTAND. I'm looking for a—

Al: OK. You don't WANT a cream puff. You want one that's BROKEN IN.

Customer: Well, I ...

Al: No need to explain. Let's move on down the line and take a gander at THIS one.

(*Brings* **Customer** *to stand in front of* **Person Two**.)

Customer: But this is another ...

Al: Another BARGAIN, believe you ME! But this one's had more EXPERIENCE. Used by a guy who TOOK what he WANTED, no apologies. He GRABBED FOR THE GUSTO, put the PEDAL to the METAL.

Customer: She looks so ... MISTREATED.

Al: Call it what you WILL, my friend. She's been put through her PACES. Steered down the PRIMROSE PATH. She's got a few DENTS. But she's got a new coat of PAINT, and she's ready to roll off the lot for a BARGAIN-BASEMENT PRICE!

Customer: I ... I'm really not looking for ...

Al: ALL RIGHT, ALL RIGHT. You don't WANT experience. You want RELIABILITY. Check THIS one out. (*Brings **Customer** to stand in front of **Person Three**.*) Just came to the lot this morning. Dependable—though the previous USER wasn't. After two fabulous years together, this trustworthy companion was DUMPED. BE-TRAYED.

Customer: WHY?

Al: Seems the previous user found something NEW. Something a little ZIPPIER, a little FANCIER. Traded this one IN—without so much as a GOODBYE.

Customer: That's TERRIBLE! But I'm really looking for . . .

Al: Don't pass up this opportunity, kid! For YOU, TODAY ONLY, I'll let you take this fine specimen off the lot for only THREE THOUSAND DOLLARS!

Customer: But I can't . . .

Al: OK, TWO THOUSAND DOLLARS.

Customer: No, no, THAT'S not what I . . .

Al: All RIGHT! FIVE HUNDRED BUCKS! But that's my FINAL OFFER!

Customer: STOP! No MORE! I can't buy what you're showing me! (*Points at **Person Three**.*) This is a PERSON! A TEENAGER! (*Points at **Persons One** and **Two**.*) They're ALL PEOPLE!

Al: Of COURSE they are! What did you EXPECT at a USED TEENAGER LOT?

Customer: Used TEENAGER lot?

Al: (*Pointing at imaginary sign*) That's right! Honest Al's is a used TEENAGER Lot!

Customer: But I'm looking for a used CAR!

Al: A WHAT?

Customer: A used CAR! I've been trying to TELL you!

Al: You mean people USE CARS?

Customer: Well, SURE.

Al: You mean they take those PRECIOUS, BEAUTIFUL MACHINES and MISTREAT them? IGNORE them? BETRAY them? As if they were mere . . . PEOPLE? I can't BELIEVE this! How could any-one be so INHUMAN as to USE a CAR? (*He takes out a handkerchief and starts sobbing and blowing his nose.*)

Customer: Yeah, well . . . I've gotta be GOING. To a used CAR lot. (*Exits.*)

Al: To think of those WONDERFUL CREATIONS, ABUSED and TOSSED AWAY . . . (*He sobs again, blows his nose, then notices that **Persons One**, **Two**, and **Three** are staring at him.*) What are YOU looking at? Get to WORK!

(**Persons One**, **Two**, and **Three** *flinch, then look sadly at the floor.* **Al** *looks offstage and brightens.*)

Al: (*As he exits*) Why, HELLO there, ma'am! Welcome to HONEST AL'S PREMIUM PRE-OWNED PRICE-CUTTERS—home of the FIVE THOUSAND-FOOT WARRANTY . . .

For Post-Play Pondering:

1. How was each of the three kids "used" by someone else? What are other ways in which kids use one another?

2. Name three kinds of "use" you think hurt a person most. Why do you think they hurt and even do damage? Of these, which two are most common among people you know?

3. Which group do you think tends to be the bigger "people user": teenagers or adults; guys or girls; parents or kids; teachers or students; Christians or non-Christians? Why?

4. What are ways in which people "used" Jesus while he was on earth? On a scale of 1 to 10 (10 being the highest), how well do you think Jesus understands the feelings of kids who are used by others today?

5. If our group were a "used teenager lot" and Jesus were the customer looking us over, what do you think he would do? Why? What might he want us to do for each other?

Other Scriptures for Study:

Psalm 68:3-6; Isaiah 53; 61:1-3; Luke 4:14-20; 1 Peter 2:17.

The Ring Thing

Topic: Love and Sex

Scripture for Study:
Genesis 2:20-25

The Scene: The living room of a teenager named **Derek**

The Simple Setup: Two chairs can represent a sofa. All other props may be pantomimed.

Other Options: If you don't want to pantomime props, you'll need a telephone and something to put it on, an onion ring in a plastic bag, a plastic bag with bits of soap in it, a cigarette (pretend to light it with an imaginary match), and a jewelry box.

The Characters:
    Derek, a smooth-talking teenage guy
    Gina, a no-nonsense teenage girl

(**Derek** and **Gina** are sitting on the sofa.)

Gina: DEREK, you didn't tell me your FOLKS would be gone tonight.

Derek: HEY, babe—I guess I FORGOT. But WE'RE here. THAT'S all that matters.

Gina: You said we were going to watch TV. Why isn't the TV ON?

Derek: It's BROKEN, babe. The WIRES melted when you GOT here. But then things are ALWAYS pretty hot when YOU'RE around, if you know what I MEAN.

Gina: How will we watch that *National Geographic* special we're supposed to see for SCHOOL?

Derek: No PROBLEM. You want WILDLIFE? I'll make sure things get pretty WILD. (*He puts his arm around her.*)

Gina: Derek, you KNOW how I feel about that.

Derek: (*Pulling back his arm*) Oh, MAN—not that RING thing again!

Gina: Derek, a wedding ring is very IMPORTANT. Getting TOO PHYSICAL before MARRIAGE is WRONG.

Derek: Gina, you're so OLD-FASHIONED! What difference does a RING make? We're in LOVE!

Gina: If you REALLY love me, you'll get me a RING.

Derek: ALL RIGHT. I got you a VERY SPECIAL RING this afternoon.

Gina: You DID? Where IS it?

Derek: In my POCKET. (*He pulls an object out of one of his pockets.*) I hope you LIKE it.

Gina: DEREK, this is an ONION ring!

Derek: I KNOW, sweetheart. Isn't it BEAUTIFUL?

Gina: Derek, an ONION ring does NOT symbolize a lifelong COMMITMENT!

Derek: Oh. Too GREASY, huh? No problem. (*He pulls another object from a different pocket.*) Here. From ME to YOU.

Gina: This is a bag of dried-up SOAP SCUM!

Derek: It's a BATHTUB RING! I scraped it out of the tub MYSELF!

Gina: GROSS! You obviously have NO RESPECT for me, Derek.

Derek: Of COURSE I do! That's why I want to offer you this VERY PER-SONAL ring. (*Parts his hair and shows her his scalp.*) SEE? Ringworm!

Gina: UGH! I'm LEAVING! (*She stands up.*)

Derek: WAIT. That was CRUDE, I know. Let me PROVE to you how SUAVE I can be. (*Takes out a cigarette, pretends to light it, and "smokes."*) I can blow SMOKE rings. (*Makes "O" shape with his lips and puffs.*) COOL, huh?

Gina: Derek, you are SO immature.

Derek: I am NOT! Want to play RING-AROUND-THE-ROSIE?

Gina: I've heard ENOUGH. You don't really care for me at ALL.

Derek: But I DO! I'd fly to the rings of SATURN for you! I'd fight for you in a BOXING ring! I'd jump through a ring of FIRE!

Gina: Then why won't you get me the kind of ring I WANT?

Derek: Gina, NOBODY waits for a WEDDING ring anymore! How about a game of RINGTOSS instead?

Gina: NO.

Derek: A copy of *Lord of the Rings*? A NOSE ring? A pair of EARRINGS?

Gina: NO! And no GYMNASTIC rings, DRUG rings, ring-BINDERS, ring-MASTERS, or RING-AROUND-THE COLLAR, either!

Derek: OK. I'll GET you what you want. A REAL ring. (*He takes the jewelry box from behind the sofa.*) My parents' JEWELRY box. It's FULL of rings. Just take your PICK.

Gina: I don't THINK so.

Derek: LOOK, sugar plum. A MOOD ring. It will turn one thousand DIFFERENT COLORS, reflecting your every precious EMOTION.

Gina: Nope.

Derek: A FRIENDSHIP ring—a sign that we will ALWAYS be together, at least until we get on each other's NERVES.

Gina: That's NOT ENOUGH.

Derek: All RIGHT. This is my mom's ENGAGEMENT ring! Surely THAT'S enough!

Gina: Sorry, Derek. Engagements can be BROKEN. And SPEAKING of broken, I'm afraid I have to BREAK UP with you.

Derek: But GINA...

Gina: You just don't UNDERSTAND, Derek. There's NO SUBSTITUTE for a WEDDING RING.

Derek: How about a TEETHING ring? Or a THREE-RING CIRCUS?

Gina: GOODBYE, Derek. (*Exits.*)

Derek: (*Calling after her*) Yeah, well, there's ONE kind of ring you won't be getting from me—a TELEPHONE ring! (*To himself*) WOMEN! Well, there are plenty more where SHE came from! (*Picks up the telephone, dials, and speaks.*) Hi, SUZIE? This is DEREK, from fifth period English. Yeah. SAY, babe—how do you like...ONION rings?

For Post-Play Pondering:

1. When you hear a "no sex before marriage" message such as the one in this skit, does it make you want to groan, cheer, snore, argue, or hide? Why?

2. How is marriage unlike other commitments like friendship, "going together," or engagement? Do you think a ring is a good symbol for marriage? What does it signify? If you had to invent another symbol that people could wear, what might it be? Why?

3. In real life, what kinds of "substitute rings" do kids offer each other as they try to convince each other to have sex?

4. If Gina had offered Derek the substitute rings, would the skit have been more or less believable? Why?

5. Why you think God forbids sex before marriage?

Other Scriptures for Study:

Song of Solomon 8:6-7; 1 Corinthians 7:1-4, 8-9; 13:4-7.

Too Many Cooks

Topic: Peer Pressure

Scripture for Study:
Romans 12:2

The Scene: The kitchen of a school cafeteria

The Simple Setup: No set is needed. All props may be pantomimed.

Other Options: Want props? The cooks could stir a "cauldron" (washtub, planter, etc.) with a broom handle. Tack a "menu" on the wall. Costumes? Each **Cook** could wear a soiled apron over casual clothes. The **New Chef** could be dressed in a clean, white shirt and pants.

The Characters:
> **Cook One**, a creepy old man or woman who makes food for a school cafeteria
> **Cook Two**, a burly, surly man or woman who works with **Cook One**
> **Cook Three**, a not-too-bright assistant who does whatever **Cooks One** and **Two** say
> **New Chef**, an innocent guy or girl fresh out of cooking school

*(**Cooks One**, **Two**, and **Three** are stirring a cauldron with a stick.)*

Cook One: Bubble, bubble, TOIL and TROUBLE...

Cook Two: Make that SCHOOL LUNCH on the DOUBLE...

Cook One: Add some SLIME and TRASH and RUBBLE...

Cook Two: Sole of SHOE and WHISKER stubble...

Cook Three: *(After a pause)* Uh...and some KETCHUP and some MUSTARD.

Cook One: Not like THAT, you NUMBSKULL! It's supposed to RHYME with "TROUBLE"!

Cook Two: Besides, ketchup and mustard are actual FOODS. We NEVER put actual FOOD in our SCHOOL-CAFETERIA LUNCHES!

Cook Three: Oh. RIGHT. Sorry.

Cook One: Let's try it AGAIN. Put into this BREW that's heating . . .

Cook Two: Heart of WORM that still is beating . . .

Cook Three: Uh . . . and a POPSICLE STICK some DOG'S been eating!

Cook One: GOOD! You may catch on YET!

(**New Chef** *enters hesitantly.*)

New Chef: EXCUSE me. Is this the KITCHEN?

Cook Two: HEY! You can't come in HERE! No STUDENTS allowed!

New Chef: Oh, I'm not a STUDENT. I'm the new CHEF.

Cook One: Did you say CHEF? You must be fresh out of COOKING SCHOOL, kid.

New Chef: That's RIGHT—I AM.

Cook One: Well, if you're going to fit IN around here, you can FORGET all that fancy CHEF stuff. You DO want to fit IN, DON'T you?

New Chef: Uh, yes. SURE. Of COURSE.

Cook Two: Then get to WORK and do whatever we SAY. GOT it?

New Chef: Well . . . OK. Just as soon as I WASH my HANDS.

Cook One: WASH your HANDS?

Cook Three: What does, "WASH YOUR HANDS" mean?

Cook One: We don't do any of THAT stuff around HERE, kid.

New Chef: But they said in COOKING SCHOOL . . .

Cook One: Did you believe everything they TOLD you in COOKING school?

Cook Two: I bet this new chef was the TEACHER'S PET!

Cook Three: Naw, we cooked the TEACHER'S PET for LUNCH last Thursday. Remember, it was a CAT about SO BIG...

Cook One: NEVER MIND! (To **New Chef**) Kid, you'll have to LOWER YOUR STANDARDS if you want to be like US. You DO want to be like US, don't you?

New Chef: Well, YES, I GUESS so.

Cook One: GOOD. Then start STIRRING this. Use a TOILET PLUNGER from the CLOSET.

New Chef: TOILET plunger? But isn't that ... UNSANITARY?

Cook Two: HEY! Do you want to be like us or NOT?

New Chef: Uh...of COURSE.

Cook One: GOOD. Now, what's on the MENU for today?

(They **all** consult an imaginary menu on the wall.)

Cook Two: Lardburgers ... fried raisins ... gelatin with cigarette butts.

Cook Three: MMM! My FAVORITE!

New Chef: Uh...I don't want to be CRITICAL or anything, but I've learned how to make some dishes that might be more...APPETIZING. Maybe I could...

Cook One: HEY! I think our little chef is AFRAID to make lardburgers!

Cook Two: YEAH! (To **New Chef**) Are you CHICKEN?

Cook Three: What's CHICKEN?

Cook One: You'd better make up your MIND, chef. Do you want to fit in or NOT?

Cook Two: YEAH! CHOOSE you this day which FOOD you will SERVE!

New Chef: I...I give UP. You're RIGHT. I WANT to be like you. You're so COOL! Those people in COOKING school were a bunch of GEEKS!

Cook One: THAT'S the spirit! Now, let's finish stirring this stuff!

*(They resume stirring, with the **New Chef** joining in.)*

Cook One: Bubble, bubble, GRIEF and WORRY...

Cook Two: Stir in something FLAT and FURRY...

Cook Three: THEN we'll call it ...

New Chef: ROAD KILL CURRY!

*(They **all** laugh. The **Cooks** congratulate the **New Chef**, shaking his or her hand and slapping him or her on the back as they **all** exit.)*

For Post-Play Pondering:

1. When you hear the words "peer pressure," what do you think of? What do you suppose most parents think of?

2. What kinds of pressure did the Cooks exert on the New Chef? In your experience, is that how peer pressure really works? Explain.

3. If you were stranded on a remote island with two non-Christians from school, would you feel more, less, or the same amount of peer pressure that you feel now? Why? After a year, would you be more like the other two or would they be more like you? Why?

4. Have you ever done something you didn't want to do, just because other people wanted you to do it? How did you feel? Have you ever refused to do something you thought was wrong, even though a friend wanted you to do it? How did that feel?

5. If all youth leaders, Sunday school teachers, and ministers agreed not to mention the subject of peer pressure for the next eight years, what might be the result for kids who are now in fifth grade? Why?

Other Scriptures for Study:

1 Kings 11:1-13; John 15:19; 1 Corinthians 15:33; 2 Corinthians 6:14-18.

Sarcastic Park

Topic: Watching Your Words

Scripture for Study:
James 3:3-8

___

The Scene: Sarcastic Park, a jungle preserve

The Simple Setup: This is a parody of the movie *Jurassic Park*. Two chairs facing the audience can represent the seats of the electric car. The **Park Ranger** needs a toy gun and should make a "thup" sound when "firing" it.

Other Options: If you want to use costumes, dress the **Riptor** and **Tyrannical Sorehead** in dark green, brown, or camouflage outfits. The **Park Ranger** could wear safari gear.

The Characters:

Michael, a teenager visitor to the park
Sheila, another teenage visitor
Announcer, an offstage voice supposedly coming through the car's speaker
Riptor, a cynical creature who tears others apart with put downs
Tyrannical Sorehead, a bad-tempered, loudmouthed creature
Park Ranger, the person in charge of park security

(**Michael** and **Sheila** sit on the chairs.)

Sheila:		Oh, MICHAEL! This is so EXCITING! We're finally in . . . SARCASTIC PARK!
Announcer:		(*From offstage*) Please keep your HANDS and ARMS inside the CAR.
Sheila:		A RECORDING—coming from this SPEAKER in the DASHBOARD!
Announcer:		(*From offstage*) Welcome to SARCASTIC PARK. You are about to meet some of the most FEARSOME CREATURES ever to roam the earth.
Michael:		Don't worry, Sheila. NOTHING could get past those ELECTRIC FENCES!

Announcer: (*From offstage*) You are now entering the domain of . . . the DEADLY RIPTOR!

Sheila: The RIPTOR! I've HEARD about that one. It can TEAR you to PIECES!

(*Suddenly the* **Riptor** *jumps onto the stage, stopping at the "electric fence."*)

Riptor: Well, look who's HERE! Two refugees from CLEARASIL CITY. Did you PIZZA-FACES order yours EXTRA UGLY or WHAT?

Sheila: OW! Those cutting remarks HURT!

Michael: Now, JUST a MINUTE, Riptor . . .

Riptor: OOH! Sir Lancelot comes to the aid of the DRAGON LADY. Take it from ME, Lance—in a battle of WITS, you'd be UNARMED!

Sheila: Thank GOODNESS—the car is MOVING again!

(*The* **Riptor** *exits.*)

Announcer: (*From offstage*) You are now LEAVING the lair of the RIPTOR. Soon you will enter the world of . . . the TYRANNICAL SOREHEAD!

Sorehead: (*Roaring offstage*) AARRGHH!

Sheila: Oh, MICHAEL!

(*The* **Sorehead** *enters and stomps angrily up to the fence.*)

Sorehead: (*Loudly*) What are YOU looking at? Do you think I LIKE having IDIOTS like you coming by every thirty seconds and BOTHERING me? Why don't you take your little GOLF CART and get OUT of here?

Sheila: B-but the car works by ITSELF. We can't . . .

Sorehead: GET LOST before I turn that HOT WHEELS REJECT into a PIE PLATE!

Michael: We're MOVING again! WHEW!

*(The **Sorehead** exits.)*

Announcer: We now proceed to a creature who SPITS STINGING REMARKS that ...

*(There is a pause. **Michael** and **Sheila** look at each other.)*

Sheila: Michael, why did the recording STOP? Why did the CAR stop?

Announcer: *(From offstage)* WARNING! Power to vehicles and electric fences has been INTERRUPTED!

Michael: We're STUCK here—and the ELECTRIC FENCES are TURNED OFF! RUN for it!

*(They get out of the car but are stopped when the **Riptor** and **Sorehead** enter.)*

Riptor: Well, well! Came back for a few more RIPS, did you?

Sorehead: I thought I told you to get LOST!

Sheila: MICHAEL! We're TRAPPED!

Announcer: *(From offstage)* MALFUNCTION! Welcome to SARCASTIC PARK! Welcome to ...

Michael: Stupid RECORDING! You're as much help as SHE is! *(Indicates **Sheila**.)*

Sheila: What's THAT supposed to mean?

Michael: Ever since we GOT here, you've been WHINING! "MICHAEL, I'm SCARED!" "MICHAEL, we're TRAPPED!"

Sheila: Well, if you KNEW what to DO, we wouldn't be IN this mess!

*(The **creatures** look at each other and scratch their heads as **Michael** and **Sheila** argue.)*

Michael: If you hadn't WHINED all year about coming to this STUPID park, we wouldn't be here at ALL!

Park Ranger: (*From offstage*) HELLO! Are any TOURISTS trapped over here?

Riptor: LOOK OUT! It's the PARK RANGER!

Sorehead: With his TRANQUILIZER GUN!

(**Creatures** *exit.* **Michael** *and* **Sheila** *stay.*)

Sheila: And ANOTHER thing! You're so DUMB that when you CHEW GUM it makes you look INTELLIGENT!

Michael: Oh, YEAH? Well, when YOU chew gum, you look like ME—only with more FACIAL HAIR.

(The **Park Ranger** *enters.*)

Park Ranger: AHA! I've CAUGHT you at LAST. Thought you'd ESCAPE, eh?

Michael: WHAT?

Park Ranger: Oh, THAT'S clever—pretending you're TOURISTS. But I HEARD those CUTTING REMARKS. If ANY creatures ever belonged in Sarcastic Park, YOU do!

Sheila: But WE'RE not . . .

Park Ranger: We'll soon have you back where you BELONG. (*He aims his gun.*) PLEASANT DREAMS!

(The **Park Ranger** *shoots* **Michael**, *then* **Sheila**. *Both slump to the floor.*)

Park Ranger: THAT'S better. (*Looks at* **Michael** *and* **Sheila**.) Poor things. I guess it's TRUE—the tongue CAN get you into a WORLD of TROU-BLE! (*Exits.*)

For Post-Play Pondering:

1. If all put downs were banned from television, which three shows would be most affected?

2. Which of the following skills are valued more in your school: making clever put downs or encouraging one another? getting back at enemies with insults or getting good grades?

3. Select two "bites" you think hurt people most: put downs about physical appearance, mental ability, moral standards, economic status, ethnic group, or athletic ability. Why do you think these put downs hurt the most?

4. Jesus occasionally used sarcasm when speaking to the religious leaders who opposed him. Does that mean it's OK for us to be sarcastic? Why or why not?

5. If each put down in our group cost the speaker 25 cents, how much would we have collected in the last year? How could we reduce hurtful remarks in our group this year?

Other Scriptures for Study:

Psalm 1; Proverbs 9:7-12; 12:18; 16:23-24; 27.

The Petrified Son

Topic: Fear of Growing Up

Scripture for Study:
Matthew 6:34

The Scene: The bedroom of the prodigal son's younger brother

The Simple Setup: Four or more chairs in a row can represent a bed. The door can be real or imagined; props should be pantomimed. If possible, bring two men's bathrobes, two towels, and two large rubber bands for instant biblical dress (use the rubber bands to secure the towels as headgear). If you can't provide these costumes, explain before the performance that the action takes place in biblical times.

Other Options: More realistic biblical dress (robes or caftans, headdresses secured with appropriate headbands, and sandals) could add to the effect.

The Characters:
> **Father**, the prodigal son's dad
> **Son**, the prodigal son's younger brother

▲ ▲ ▲ ▲ ▲ ▲ ▲ ▲

*(The **Son** is lying on his bed, turning the pages of a book. The **Father** knocks on the **Son's** door.)*

Father: HELLO, Son! It's DAD! May I come IN?

Son: Uh, JUST A MINUTE! (*He tries to hide the book under the bed.*) Hold ON! (*He lies back down, trying to look casual.*) OK!

Father: Hi. Could I TALK with you?

Son: SURE, Dad.

Father: (*Sitting on the end of the bed*) Son, your MOTHER and I were walking the GOATS down by the TEMPLE the other day, and ... (*He looks down and notices something.*) What's THIS sticking out from under your BED?

Son: Uh, NOTHING!

Father: A BOOK? (*Reaching down and picking it up*) It's *Goldilocks and the Three Camels!* SON, why are you reading a CHILDREN'S book?

Son: I—I'M still a child, sort of.

Father: But you're EIGHTEEN YEARS OLD! Why, when your OLDER BROTHER was eighteen...

Son: I KNOW! He was demanding his INHERITANCE so he could go out into the WORLD. EVERYBODY knows the story of the PRODIGAL SON!

Father: Yes, I suppose SO. ANYWAY, your MOTHER and I were thinking that... (*He looks at the wall and frowns.*) Son, what are those POSTERS on your wall?

Son: That one's KERMIT THE OX and MISS FIGGY. Those are MICKEY AND MINNIE LOCUST. And there's BARNEY THE DONKEY.

Father: Son, why don't you have posters of FAMOUS MUSICIANS or ATH-LETES? When your OLDER BROTHER was your age, he had...

Son: I KNOW! He had HALF your ESTATE, and he took it to a FAR COUNTRY and wasted it in WILD LIVING. Then he fed PIGS and wished he could have some of the CORNCOBS they were eating. I've heard the story a MILLION TIMES! After all, I'm the prodigal son's LITTLE BROTHER!

Father: And THAT'S why I'm HERE. Your MOTHER and I have decided that you should have YOUR part of the inheritance.

Son: But I don't WANT it!

Father: Son, it's time for you to go out into the WORLD. You can't stay in your room FOREVER!

Son: Why NOT?

Father: You're a MAN now, Son. You need to get out there and make your OWN way... make your OWN decisions... make your OWN bed!

Son: But I want to stay HERE! I want to play with my BLOCKS! I want to play with my PET FATTED CALF, SPOT! (*Calling*) HERE, Spot! HERE, boy!

Father: Uh...Son...ABOUT SPOT. Remember that big PARTY we had when your OLDER BROTHER came home? When we KILLED A FATTED CALF and ATE it?

Son: Yeah...what ABOUT it?

Father: Uh...THAT CALF WAS...(*sighing*) oh, NEVER MIND. Son, I know GROWING UP is hard to do. But we ALL have to do it. You need to get your CAMEL DRIVER'S license. You could go off to COLLEGE and become a SHEPHERD. Or a GOAT HERDER. Or a FARMER. You have so many CHOICES!

Son: But what if I make the WRONG choice? I don't want to end up in some PIGSTY, wishing I could eat CORNCOBS!

Father: YOU'LL make BETTER choices, Son. I'm SURE of it.

Son: And if I FAIL, will you always be waiting for me with OPEN ARMS and a FATTED CALF?

Father: Uh...I GUESS so. Except that we've, uh, RUN OUT OF fatted calves. Maybe we could have a FATTED CHEESE SANDWICH.

Son: And will you always leave my ROOM the way it is NOW?

Father: Well, NO. Your MOTHER and I are planning to move to a CONDO.

Son: A CONDO? But where will I put all the things I made out of CLAY-DOUGH? And my *Sesame Seed Street* VIDEO collection?

Father: It's time to put those things BEHIND you, Son. It's time to LEAVE HOME.

Son: But I CAN'T!

Father: I'm SORRY, Son. It's TIME. I'll have your INHERITANCE ready for you in the MORNING. (He *stands to leave.*) I'll just . . . (He *listens, frowning.*) What's that SOUND?

Son: Oh. (He *picks up an object from the floor.*) I left my COMPACT DISCUS player on.

Father: Your CD player? GOOD! Now THERE'S something I would expect a young MAN to use. Good night, Son. I'll see you in the morning. (*Exits.*)

Son: (*To himself*) I wonder what he'd say if he knew I was listening to songs from the LAMB CHOP'S PLAYTENT show. (He *turns off the imaginary CD player.*) Nobody UNDERSTANDS. Nobody EVER understands—except my pet fatted CALF, SPOT. I'll go TALK to him. THEN I'll feel better. (He *stands to leave.*) Oh, SPOT! SPOT! HERE, boy! Where ARE you, Spot? (*Exits.*)

For Post-Play Pondering:

1. What would be the advantages of always staying at your present age? What would be the disadvantages?

2. If the average teenager has mixed feelings about growing up, what percentage of those feelings do you think are fearful and what percentage are eager?

3. When it comes to growing up, do you think Christian kids are more confident, less confident, or just as confident as non-Christian kids? Why? Do you think there should be a difference? Why or why not?

4. What are three mistakes you've seen older people make that you'd like to avoid? What will you do to avoid them?

5. If you could get written assurance from God about one aspect of your future, what would you want it to be? How would that assurance compare to Jesus' promise, "I am with you always" (Matthew 28:20)?

Other Scriptures for Study:

Luke 15:11-32; John 14:27; 1 Corinthians 13:11.

The Waiting Room

Topic: Death

Scripture for Study:
Luke 12:16-21

The Scene: A high school biology classroom at night

The Simple Setup: No set is needed if the group will be able to see the "frogs" who are crouching on the floor. If visibility will be a problem, set up a couple of long, sturdy tables for the actors to crouch on.

Other Options: A few costume additions could help to identify the characters. Try a backward baseball cap or beer-logo hat for **Loud Frog**, a goofy T-shirt for **Giggly Frog**, and a Hawaiian shirt for **Surfer Frog**.

The Characters:

    Loud Frog, a party-hearty amphibian
    Giggly Frog, an amphibian who can't seem to take anything seriously
    Surfer Frog, a spaced-out amphibian who talks using stereotypical California surf
            lingo
    Worried Frog, a thoughtful and nervous amphibian

*(**All** except **Worried** crouch side by side on the floor or table. **Worried** lies asleep.)*

Giggly:		RIBBIT! RIBBIT! (*Giggles.*)
Surfer:		RIBBIT! RIBBIT, dude!
Loud:		RIBBIT! RIBBIT! (*Burps.*)
Surfer:		THAT was SOME BURP, dude! I didn't know frogs COULD burp!
Worried:		(*Waking up*) HEY! Wha—what's going ON?
Loud:		Well, if it isn't SLEEPING BEAUTY!
Giggly:		Hee, hee! You've been out like a LIGHT!

Worried: How—how long have we BEEN here?

Surfer: We don't KNOW, dude. We were out cold OURSELVES until a couple of MINUTES ago.

Worried: Where ARE we?

Loud: Who KNOWS? Who CARES? Let's PARTY!

Worried: HOLD it! Last thing I remember, we were in the SWAMP. All of a sudden, this BIG HAND reached down and put me in a JAR. It SMELLED funny. Something must have KNOCKED me OUT.

Surfer: I remember THAT! What a RUSH, man!

Worried: And now here we ARE, in . . . some kind of CAGE. In a big, dark ROOM. What's the writing on that DOOR over there?

Surfer: (*Reading a letter at a time*) B-I-O-L-O-G-Y-L-A-B.

Loud: That spells . . . PARTY TIME!

Worried: No—it spells "BIOLOGY LAB." I think my GRANDMOTHER warned me about that once. But I don't remember WHY.

Loud: Doesn't MATTER! Let's find something to DRINK!

Giggly and Surfer: PAR-TY! PAR-TY!

Loud: THERE'S a bottle, right next to our CAGE!

Worried: WAIT a minute! My grandmother told me frogs go INTO places like this—but they never come OUT again. She said NOBODY gets out of here ALIVE.

Surfer: WHOA! You mean like DYING, dude?

Loud: Hey, I'M not gonna die, man. That's for OLD frogs!

Worried: But don't you SEE? We're TRAPPED! Any time, even tomorrow morning, one of those big hands could come in and GRAB us!

Surfer: No WAY! We'll be safe here for YEARS and YEARS. We can even build a bigger CAGE.

Giggly: We can have TADPOLES of our OWN! (*Giggles.*)

Loud: And we can PARTY!

Worried: STOP! Don't you SEE? There's no way OUT!

Loud: So WHAT? Let's get that bottle and PARTY DOWN!

Giggly: What's that WORD on the LABEL of the bottle?

Surfer: (*Reading a letter at a time*) F-O-R-M-A-L-D-E-H-Y-D-E.

Worried: FORMALDEHYDE...I think my grandmother told me about that, too, but...I can't remember.

Loud: Doesn't MATTER. It's something to DRINK—so let's DRINK it!

(**All** *except* **Worried** *reach as if through a cage and pull the cap off the bottle.*)

Surfer: Bottoms UP, dudes!

Worried: WAIT! You can't ...

Loud: Out of the WAY, you TOAD!

(**All** *except* **Worried** *take turns drinking directly from the bottle.*)

Surfer: WHOO, dude! That's powerful STUFF!

Giggly: It tickles my NOSE! (*Giggles.*)

Loud: It makes me want to...(*suddenly getting a glazed look*) SLOW...DOWN.

Giggly: Ooh...what's...HAPPENING?

Surfer: I feel like...I'm SINKING...

Worried: I tried to WARN you!

Loud: Ribbit...ribbit...

(**All** *except* **Worried** *fall to the floor, dead.*)

Worried: FORMALDEHYDE! NOW I remember...EVERYTHING. (*Takes a drink from the bottle, then sits, staring into space.*) Eat...drink...and be merry...for tomorrow...we DISSECT! (*Slumps to the floor, dead.*)

For Post-Play Pondering:

1. Which of these frogs best represents the attitudes toward death held by most kids you know? Which best represents your attitude? Why?

2. What are four ways in which you're *sure* the death of a person is different from the death of a frog? What are two ways in which you *think* they're different but aren't sure?

3. What "warnings" have the following sources given you about death: (a) teachers and police, (b) the Bible, (c) parents, and (d) friends? Which sources do you trust most? Why?

4. As far as you're concerned, is this life most like the waiting room in (a) a dentist's office, (b) a principal's office, (c) a restaurant, or (d) an auto repair shop? Why?

5. What five things would you most like to do before you die? What five things do you think God would most like you to do before you die?

Other Scriptures for Study:
Ecclesiastes 3:1-14; Philippians 1:21-26; James 4:13-17.

Extra!

Topic: The Good News of Jesus

Scripture for Study:
1 Corinthians 1:18-31

The Scene: A street corner

The Simple Setup: No set is needed. The **Newsboy** (who can be male or female) will need a stack of newspapers (not necessarily all the same edition). **Passersby** may pantomime giving their money to the **Newsboy**.

Other Options: The **Newsboy** could wear an oversized coat and baseball cap for a "street urchin" look. The **Passersby** might also wear coats to indicate that they're outside.

The Characters:
Newsboy, a kid who sells papers on a street corner
Passerby One
Passerby Two
Passerby Three
Passerby Four
Passerby Five

*(The **Newsboy** stands next to a stack of newspapers and holds one up in the air.)*

Newsboy: EXTRA! EXTRA! Read all ABOUT it! BABY Born in BETHLEHEM!

*(**Passerby One** enters and walks past without paying attention, then exits.)*

Newsboy: KING Comes to Lowly STABLE! HEY, get your PAPER!

*(**Passerby Two** enters slowly, looking around.)*

Newsboy: EXTRA! EXTRA! GET your paper HERE! Amazing STAR Appears in Eastern SKY! Heavenly CHOIR Sings to SHEPHERDS! WISE MEN Travel From AFAR!

Passerby Two: EXCUSE me . . . Does your paper have the story about that MOVIE STAR who walked off the set when she ran out of HAIR SPRAY?

Newsboy: Uh…NO.

Passerby Two: Oh. Well, NEVER MIND.

(*Passerby Two* exits. The *Newsboy* sighs and tries again.)

Newsboy: EXTRA! Man Turns WATER Into WINE!

(*Passersby Three* and *Four* enter, pretending to talk with each other.)

Newsboy: Ten Lepers HEALED! Lazarus Recovers From FATAL ILLNESS! Get your paper HERE, folks!

Passerby Three: (*To Newsboy*) Do you have the REALLY big story? About the lady who found a POTATO shaped like the Brazilian HOCKEY team?

Newsboy: Well, NO.

Passerby Four: What kind of paper IS that? Don't you have any NEWS in it?

(*Passersby Three* and *Four* exit. The *Newsboy* shakes his or her head and tries again.)

Newsboy: HEY, read all about it INSIDE! Long-Promised MESSIAH Arrives! Triumphant ENTRY Parade Greeted by Cheering CROWDS!

(*Passerby Five* enters and listens.)

Newsboy: EXTRA! Messiah Condemned in ILLEGAL TRIAL! SCANDAL Taints Roman GOVERNOR!

Passerby Five: Speaking of SCANDAL, how about that messy DIVORCE involving a certain U.S. SENATOR and a glamorous LIBRARIAN from Slug Harbor, New Hampshire?

Newsboy: Uh…I hadn't HEARD about it.

Passerby Five: And you call THAT a NEWSPAPER? (*Exits.*)

(The *Newsboy*, irritated, tries again.)

Newsboy: Get your PAPER! Messiah EXECUTED on CROSS! Earthquake ROCKS Jerusalem! Come ON, folks! Read all ABOUT it!

(**Passerby One** *enters again from the other side, walks past without paying attention, and exits.*)

Newsboy: HEY, what's the MATTER with you people? Don't you recognize the STORY OF THE CENTURY when you hear it?

(**Passerby One** *enters again.*)

Passerby One: Did you say the STORY OF THE CENTURY?

Newsboy: YES!

Passerby One: You mean the one about the guy in AUSTRALIA who can play THE BRADY BUNCH THEME on the PIPE ORGAN with his TOES?

Newsboy: NO!

Passerby One: Well, then, FORGET it. (*Exits.*)

(The **Newsboy** *glares after him or her, then tries one more time.*)

Newsboy: OK! Maybe those stories weren't IMPRESSIVE enough for you. But there's no way you can resist THIS one! (*Pauses to roll up his or her sleeves, then calls out more loudly than ever.*) EXTRA! EXTRA! Man RISES From the DEAD! Massive STONE Rolled Away by ANGELS! Man WALKS Through WALLS! DEAD Man LIVES Again! ETERNAL LIFE Guaranteed to All Who BELIEVE!

(The **Newsboy** *waits hopefully, but nothing happens.* **Newsboy** *throws down the paper, disgusted.*)

Newsboy: I give UP! (*He or she thinks for a moment, folds his or her arms, and calls out a made-up headline.*) EXTRA! TALK SHOW HOST Reveals Secrets of BALSA-WOOD DIET!

(**All Passersby** *enter excitedly, get out their money, and gather around the* **Newsboy**.)

Newsboy: Face of GILLIGAN Appears in CLOUDS Over South Sea ISLAND!

Passerby One: Now THERE'S a story!

Passerby Two: I'll take TWO copies!

Newsboy: THREE-HEADED MAN Gives Birth to FOUR-HEADED SEA MONKEYS!

Passerby Three: OOH! SEA monkeys!

Newsboy: ELVIS Sighted Eating GIANT, ALIEN UFO DOUGHNUT!

Passerby Five: THAT I can believe!

(**All Passersby** *give money to the* **Newsboy**, *take papers, and exit.*)

Newsboy: (*Sighing*) I guess the GOOD NEWS...just isn't GOOD enough anymore! (*The* **Newsboy** *shrugs and exits.*)

For Post-Play Pondering:

1. If Jesus' resurrection had happened one month ago, do you think it would (a) still be in the news, (b) qualify as one of the year's top stories, or (c) be made into a TV-movie docudrama? Why?

2. What reactions do you think the Newsboy might get (a) in front of your school, (b) with a group of your friends, (c) outside your church?

3. Have you ever tried to explain to someone what the "good news" about Jesus is? What happened?

4. Which of the following do you think most people find hardest to believe: (a) that Jesus is God's Son, (b) that Jesus performed miracles, (c) that Jesus died for their sins, (d) that Jesus rose from the dead, or (e) that they need to put their faith in Jesus personally? Why?

5. What might happen if all Christians gave up trying to convince others to listen to the good news? What do you think is the best way to get people to listen?

Other Scriptures for Study:

Matthew 11:2-6, 20-30; Mark 8:31-33; John 20; Romans 1:20-25; 1 Corinthians 15.

The Birthday Boy

Topic: Christmas

Scripture for Study:
Luke 2:1-20

The Scene: The bedroom of **Miriam**, a teenage girl from biblical times

The Simple Setup: Two rows of four chairs (each row representing one bed) should be placed end to end so that the actors can sit and lie on them.

Other Options: Biblical dress (robes, sandals, and so on) might help to set the scene.

The Characters:
> **Miriam**, a girl who sometimes baby-sits the baby Jesus
> **Joanna**, her friend

(**Miriam** and **Joanna** are sitting on beds.)

Miriam: JOANNA—I'm, like, SO glad you could sleep OVER! I've been so BUSY I hardly SEE you anymore.

Joanna: No LIE! I can't BELIEVE all the stuff you're DOING, Miriam. You're the head CHEERLEADER at Bethlehem Middle School. You're on the GRAIN-GRINDING team...

Miriam: And I've got all these CHORES. Like sweeping the FLOOR. I HATE these dirt floors! I wish somebody would invent LINOLEUM or something.

Joanna: And on top of THAT, you do so much BABY-SITTING!

Miriam: It PAYS pretty well. I can get a DRACHMA [*pronounced* DROCK-*ma*] an HOUR sometimes.

Joanna: WOW! I baby-sat for that stingy Mrs. SAPPHIRA last week, and SHE gave me only a couple of MITES. And that KID of hers is such a BRAT! He wouldn't go to bed unless I let him watch the SUNSET first.

Miriam: YEAH, I get some brats, TOO. But not little JESUS.

Joanna: Oh, is HE the one who was born in a BARN? He is SO CUTE!

Miriam: And so WELL-BEHAVED. The CATTLE can be LOWING outside, and he awakes—but no CRYING he makes!

Joanna: Did his parents finally get him a CRIB? I felt SORRY for him, sleeping away in that MANGER.

Miriam: Of COURSE they did. He's eleven months OLD, you know!

Joanna: He IS? Well, then his first BIRTHDAY is coming up!

Miriam: That's RIGHT! Oh, what should we DO for his BIRTHDAY?

Joanna: Let's get a TREE.

Miriam: WHAT?

Joanna: A TREE. Let's CUT DOWN a TREE, DRAG it INSIDE, and HANG things on it.

Miriam: WHY?

Joanna: I don't know. It was just an IDEA.

Miriam: Kind of a STRANGE idea, if you ask ME. Let's think about what HE might like to do.

Joanna: Oh, I know! My Uncle BENJAMIN could come over.

Miriam: What FOR?

Joanna: Uncle Benjamin has this LONG, WHITE BEARD and a BIG BELLY. He could dress up in red and white clothes and yell, "HO, HO, HO!"

Miriam: Would little JESUS like that?

Joanna: Probably NOT. But wouldn't it be great ANYWAY?

Miriam: WHY?

Joanna: Beats ME. Just thought I'd SUGGEST it.

Miriam: Let's think about how we could HONOR Jesus on his birthday. He has so many GOOD QUALITIES.

Joanna: How about eating so many CANDIES and COOKIES that we get SICK?

Miriam: How does THAT honor JESUS?

Joanna: Yeah, forget THAT. Let's SEE... We could hang up LEAVES and BERRIES, and whoever stands UNDER them has to KISS somebody!

Miriam: What are you TALKING about?

Joanna: I'm not SURE. Hey, I know—we could SING SONGS about SNOW!

Miriam: What's SNOW?

Joanna: I have NO IDEA.

Miriam: Joanna—maybe I should just plan this MYSELF.

Joanna: No, WAIT—I've GOT it! It's so OBVIOUS! (*Pauses.*) PRESENTS!

Miriam: Of COURSE! You ALWAYS give people presents on their BIRTH-DAYS. What do you think JESUS might like?

Joanna: NO, NO. I don't mean for HIM. I mean for US.

Miriam: You think we should give EACH OTHER presents on HIS birthday? WHY?

Joanna: Because we LIKE presents!

Miriam: OH. Yeah, I guess that makes SENSE.

Joanna: SURE it does. I'll give YOU a list of the presents I want.

Miriam: And I'LL give you MY list.

Joanna: This will be so much FUN! It'll be the BEST birthday EVER!

Miriam: Birthday? WHOSE birthday?

Joanna: Uh…I don't REMEMBER.

Miriam: Me NEITHER. (*Yawns.*) Well, I'm getting kind of SLEEPY.

Joanna: Me, TOO. Good night.

Miriam: GOOD NIGHT, Joanna. And…HAPPY HOLIDAYS!

(*They lie down and go to sleep.*)

► For Post-Play Pondering:

1. What's your idea of a great birthday party for yourself?

2. What would be the best way for your friends to honor you if they couldn't spend more than $5 total?

3. Do you think Jesus wants people to celebrate his birthday? Why or why not?

4. In what ways should Christmas be for Jesus' benefit? In what ways should it benefit us?

5. Which three Christmas traditions make the most sense to you? the least sense?

6. How could our group celebrate Jesus' birth without using a tree, presents, refreshments, or even reading the "Christmas story" in Luke 2:1-20? How might doing that affect our attitudes about Christmas?

7. For the moment, set aside all our modern Christmas customs and think only of the fact that Jesus came to earth. Why did He come? What do you think motivated God to send his Son? What does this mean to you personally?

Other Scriptures for Study:

Psalm 98; Mark 9:2-7; Luke 1:46-55, 67-80.

The Big Picture

Topic: Forgiveness

Scripture for Study:
Matthew 18:21-35

The Scene: A movie set

The Simple Setup: A chair is needed for **Scorekeeper**.

Other Options: **Scorekeeper** could sit in a canvas-backed director's chair. The **Camera Person** could use a video camera on a tripod. **C.B. DeVine** could be dressed in a suit.

The Characters:
> **Martin Scorekeeper**, the cranky movie director
> **Flint Eastwind**, the male movie star
> **Beryl Strep**, the female movie star
> **Camera Person**
> **C.B. DeVine**, the movie producer

*(**Scorekeeper** sits in a chair next to the **Camera Person**, who looks through the viewfinder of a movie camera that is pointed at **Flint** and **Beryl**.)*

Scorekeeper: All RIGHT, everybody! Quiet on the SET! This is a Martin SCOREKEEPER film, so every second COUNTS!

Flint: Martin, I don't UNDERSTAND this scene. What's my MOTIVATION?

Scorekeeper: Your motivation is that I'm in a HURRY! I don't care if you ARE Flint Eastwind and Beryl Strep! The two of you are costing me fifty thousand dollars a MINUTE! So start ACTING!

Camera Person: *The Day the EARTH Tipped Over*—Scene FORTY-TWO, Take ONE!

Scorekeeper: ACTION!

Flint: Oh, my DARLING—no matter HOW this situation turns out, you must always remember that little TUNA I taught you . . .

Scorekeeper: CUT!

Flint: What's WRONG?

Scorekeeper: You said "TUNA"! It's "TUNE"! You taught her a SONG, not a FISH!

Flint: Oh. Sorry.

Scorekeeper: Try it AGAIN!

Camera Person: *The Day the EARTH Tipped Over*—Scene FORTY-TWO, Take TWO!

Scorekeeper: ACTION!

Flint: Oh, my DARLING—no matter how this SANDWICH turns out—

Scorekeeper: CUT! It's "SITUATION," not "SANDWICH"!

Flint: But, Martin, I'm so HUNGRY! I can't stop thinking of FOOD! Can't we break for LUNCH?

Scorekeeper: NO! Time is MONEY! Remember, I'm KEEPING SCORE! Do it AGAIN! And THIS time, get it RIGHT!

Camera Person: *The Day the EARTH Tipped Over*—Scene FORTY-TWO, Take THREE!

Scorekeeper: ACTION!

Flint: Oh, my DUMPLING...

Scorekeeper: CUT! CUT! You're FIRED, Eastwind! You're HISTORY! Now, get off my...

(**C.B. DeVine** *enters.*)

Beryl: (*To* **Flint**) LOOK! It's the PRODUCER—Mr. C.B. DEVINE! I've HEARD of him, but I've never actually SEEN him!

C.B.: SO, Martin! How's the PICTURE going?

Scorekeeper: Not so GOOD, C.B. These lousy ACTORS keep blowing their LINES! I've had to do THREE TAKES of this scene ALREADY!

C.B.: THREE? Is that ALL?

Scorekeeper: Well, how many chances should I GIVE them? SEVEN?

C.B.: NOPE. Seventy TIMES seven.

Scorekeeper: WHAT? That's FOUR HUNDRED AND NINETY!

C.B.: DON'T worry. I'LL pay for it.

Scorekeeper: But C.B.! At thirty seconds a take, that's FOURTEEN THOUSAND SEVEN HUNDRED SECONDS!

C.B.: I KNOW, Martin. YOU'RE keeping score. But I'M not. After all, should I keep track of how much I lost on those OTHER pictures you directed?

Scorekeeper: Well . . .

C.B.: Like A Day in the Life of a PAPER PLATE?

Scorekeeper: Uh . . . NO. I'm . . . ready when YOU are, C.B.!

C.B.: GOOD! PLACES, everybody! And have a nice day. (Exits.)

Scorekeeper: OK, OK! Take it from the TOP!

Camera Person: The Day the EARTH Tipped Over—Scene FORTY-TWO, Take FOUR!

Scorekeeper: ACTION!

Flint: Oh, my DARLING—no matter HOW this situation turns out, you must ALWAYS remember that little TUNE I taught you. Do you remember it?

Beryl: Of COURSE I do, my sweet!

Scorekeeper: CUT! PRINT it! That's PERFECT! Well, I guess we ALL feel better now—thanks to C.B. I really shouldn't have been so...

Camera Person: Oops.

Scorekeeper: What do you MEAN "OOPS"?

Camera Person: I...uh...forgot to put any FILM in the camera. We'll...have to do the whole thing OVER.

Flint and Beryl: (*Chasing the* **Camera Person**, *who runs*) KILL him! Kill him NOW!

Camera Person: HEY! I've got FOUR HUNDRED AND EIGHTY-NINE CHANCES left, remember?

(*The* **Camera Person** *exits, pursued by* **Flint** *and* **Beryl***.*)

Scorekeeper: Hmm. They really should be more FORGIVING. Keeping SCORE makes one so TENSE...don't you THINK? (*Exits, whistling.*)

For Post-Play Pondering:

1. Who do you think has forgiven you the most times in your life? Who do you think you've forgiven most?

2. If people were paid $10 for each time they forgave someone, how might the world be different? Is there any payment or reward for forgiving?

3. Which of the following would you find hardest to forgive if it happened to you: (a) someone smashes the windshield of your car, (b) someone spreads a false rumor about you, or (c) someone beats you out of a scholarship by cheating? Why?

4. What's the worst thing that could happen if you kept forgiving someone? What's the best thing that could happen?

5. How would you respond to this statement: "It was easy for Jesus to say, 'Forgive people seventy times seven.' He never actually had to do it."?

Other Scriptures for Study:

Genesis 50:15-21; Matthew 6:9-15; Ephesians 4:31-32.

The Pewgitive

Topic: Commitment

Scripture for Study:
Acts 2:42-47

The Scene: Nowhere in particular

The Simple Setup: This is a parody of the movie *The Fugitive*. You'll need a couple of pews (or rows of chairs to represent them). The **Leader** should have a large bandage over one of his or her ears. The **Kazoo Player** could hum with or without a real kazoo. The **Announcer** and **Kazoo Player** should be offstage, either seen or unseen. **Nimble** will need a paper wad in his pocket. Make sure the **Announcer** knows that "Pewgitive" is pronounced "pew-ji-tive."

Other Options: The **Announcer** and **Kazoo Player** could use a live microphone.

The Characters:
> **Announcer**, stern and deep-voiced
> **Kazoo Player**
> **Richard Nimble**, a teenager on the run
> **One-Eared Youth Leader**, male or female
> **Pat**, a friendly teenager, male or female
> **Chris**, another friendly teenager, male or female

▲ ▲ ▲ ▲ ▲ ▲ ▲ ▲

Announcer: (*From offstage*) The PEWGITIVE!

(The **Kazoo Player** *hums ominous-sounding music.*)

Announcer: (*From offstage*) His name is RICHARD NIMBLE...

(The **Kazoo Player** *hums more ominous-sounding music.*)

Announcer: (*From offstage*) Enough music! (*Music stops.*)  His name is RICHARD NIMBLE...

(**Richard** *enters and runs in place, nervously looking over his shoulder from time to time.*)

Announcer: (*From offstage*) A TEENAGER, he runs from YOUTH GROUP to YOUTH GROUP... unwilling to COMMIT. He is pursued by a ONE-EARED YOUTH LEADER...

*(The **Leader** enters and runs in place behind **Richard**, looking around, puzzled.)*

Leader: RICHARD! Richard NIMBLE! Where ARE you?

Announcer: *(From offstage)* RUNNING, always RUNNING, Nimble hides behind PEW after PEW.

*(**Richard** ducks behind a pew.)*

Announcer: *(From offstage)* And THAT is why they call him . . . The PEWGITIVE!

*(The **Kazoo Player** hums more ominous-sounding music.)*

Announcer: *(From offstage)* HEY!

Kazoo Player: *(From offstage)* OK, OK!

Announcer: *(From offstage)* TONIGHT'S episode . . . "RUNNING ON EMPTY"!

Leader: *(No longer running)* RICHARD! Where ARE you? The YOUTH MEET-ING is starting! All your FRIENDS will be there! *(Pauses.)* You'll have a GREAT TIME, Richard! We're going to have PIZZA!

Richard: *(Still hiding)* What KIND of pizza?

Leader: WHAT? You'll have to SPEAK UP! I've only got ONE EAR!

Richard: *(Louder)* I said, what KIND of pizza?

Leader: PEPPERONI! Your FAVORITE! PLEASE come back, Richard!

Richard: If I come BACK, you'll just try to get me INVOLVED!

Leader: Come BACK, Richard! The group NEEDS you!

Richard: I . . . DON'T . . . CARE! *(He takes a wad of paper out of his pocket and throws it across the stage, distracting the attention of the **Leader**.)*

Leader: Richard, are you over HERE?

(*Running after the paper wad, the* **Leader** *exits.*)

Richard: (*Standing*) GOOD. (*He runs in place again.*) I've GOT to find a group where I won't have to COMMIT. Nobody's making a prisoner out of ME!

(**Pat** *and* **Chris** *enter and pretend to talk with each other on one side of the stage.*)

Richard: THERE! A GROUP I can visit! (*He walks over to* **Pat** *and* **Chris**.)

Pat: HI! Welcome to our GROUP!

Chris: I'm CHRIS, and this is PAT. What's YOUR name?

Richard: Uh…It's NOT RICHARD NIMBLE. It's…uh…TRIMBLE. No. TRUMBLE. TIM Trumble. NO. It's ED. REALLY.

Pat: Nice to MEET you, Ed. Have you BEEN here before?

Richard: NO. I mean YES. I mean, I was here, but nobody ELSE was. It was the middle of the NIGHT. I OVERSLEPT.

Chris: You look FAMILIAR, Ed. Where have I seen your FACE?

Richard: Uh…on a PENNY. That's MY FACE on the penny. Not on ALL of them. Just SOME of them. The BIG ones that look like NICKELS. YEAH.

Pat: Well, I think you'll LIKE our group. We go to the MOUNTAINS sometimes. Last summer we had a MISSIONS trip.

Chris: Would you like to sign up for the RETREAT? There's a SHEET right over…

Richard: OH no you don't! You're trying to make me COMMIT myself! You'll never get me ALIVE! (*He exits, running.*)

Chris: Was it something I SAID?

(The **Leader** enters, out of breath.)

Leader: EXCUSE me! Did you see a guy running through here? About SO TALL?

Pat: You mean ED TRUMBLE?

Leader: WHAT? I can't HEAR you!

Pat and Chris: (Together, pointing) He went THAT way!

Leader: (Calling after **Richard**) RICHARD! We're having ICE CREAM SUNDAES! Richard, come BACK! (Exits.)

Pat: BOY—that guy is WANTED!

(**Pat** and **Chris** exit.)

Announcer: (From offstage) And so Richard Nimble RUNS. Never at HOME. Always HIDING. Looking for the PERFECT GROUP—one that offers EVERYTHING and demands NOTHING of . . . The PEWGITIVE! (Pauses.) I SAID . . . The PEWGITIVE!

Kazoo Player: (From offstage) Oh. Right.

(The **Kazoo Player** hums a closing fanfare.)

For Post-Play Pondering:

1. Let's say that three experiences from Richard Nimble's past made him unwilling to stick with a youth group. What might they be?

2. If you were a youth group leader, why would you want kids to be committed to the group? Do you think it matters to anyone other than leaders? Why or why not?

3. How committed to the group would you say each of the following kids is (on a scale of 1 to 10, with 10 being the highest): (a) one who always asks, "Who else will be there?"

before deciding whether to attend; (b) one who attends every meeting and spends the time snickering in the back row; (c) one who misses some meetings but prays for others in the group; and (d) one who attends only "fun" events? Explain.

4. Do you think God is committed to *our* group or to youth groups in *general*? Explain.

5. If everyone in our group had the same commitment to the group that you do, what might our group be like six months from now?

Other Scriptures for Study:

Ecclesiastes 4:7-10; Matthew 25:14-46; Galatians 6:2-5; Hebrews 6:9-12; 13:15-17.

All in Your Mind

Topic: Entertainment Choices

Scripture for Study:
Colossians 2:8

The Scene: The bedroom of **Randy**, a teenager

The Simple Setup: One chair is needed. Props may be pantomimed. The door may be real or imaginary.

Other Options: A working stereo, TV, and video game could be set up if desired.

The Characters:
  Randy, a teenage guy or girl addicted to entertainment
  Mom, the weary and worried mother of **Randy**

▲ ▲ ▲ ▲ ▲ ▲ ▲ ▲

(*Randy* sits on a chair, staring into space and moving to the beat of music we can't hear.)

Mom: (*Shouting from offstage*) RANDY!

Randy: (*Shouting back*) You got the RIGHT ONE, baby, UH-HUH!

Mom: Turn down that NOISE!

Randy: It may sound FUNNY, but it's STILL ROCK'N'ROLL to ME!

Mom: Randy, this has GOT to STOP! I'm coming IN there!

Randy: Come on DOWN! HERE comes the JUDGE, HERE comes the JUDGE!

(**Mom** *opens the door.*)

Mom: You've got the STEREO going, AND the TV, AND a video game!

Randy: *Entertainment* TONIGHT!

Mom: May I come IN?

Randy: Welcome to my NIGHTMARE. Don't step on my BLUE SUEDE SHOES. All I wanna DO is HAVE some FUN.

(**Mom** *enters and heads for the stereo.*)

Mom: I'm turning this OFF. And THIS, and THIS.

Randy: Can't touch THIS. Don't touch that DIAL! I want my MTV!

(**Mom** *turns off the stereo, TV, and video game.*)

Mom: THERE. Randy, we have GOT to TALK.

Randy: It's *Family Feud*! MORTAL KOMBAT! Go ahead—MAKE my DAY.

Mom: Randy, all you ever do is listen to MUSIC, watch TV, play VIDEO GAMES, and go to the MOVIES. You've GOT to get out of this ROOM more often—and not just to see more MOVIES!

Randy: I LOVE this place!

Mom: Do you even know what the WEATHER is like outside?

Randy: It's a BEAUTIFUL DAY in the NEIGHBORHOOD. High today of seventy three, low tonight in the MID-FIFTIES. We'll be back with SPORTS, right after THIS.

Mom: Do you even know what day of the WEEK it is?

Randy: Live from New York…it's SATURDAY NIGHT!

Mom: Honey, I'm WORRIED about you. All this entertainment MUST be having an EFFECT on you.

Randy: Don't WORRY, baby. Raise your HAND if you're SURE.

Mom: I AM sure! What about the words of those SONGS you listen to? They promote SEX OUTSIDE OF MARRIAGE. THAT'S not the kind of love Christians believe in.

Randy: What's LOVE got to do with it? It can't be WRONG if it feels so RIGHT. I'm about to lose control, and I think I LIKE it.

Mom: SEE? You're picking up the WRONG VALUES!

Randy: Let it BE, let it BE, let it BE, let it BE. I would do ANYTHING for love, but I won't do THAT.

Mom: And what about the TV you watch? All those COMMERCIALS make you want MORE AND MORE THINGS and draw you away from what REALLY matters.

Randy: Because I'm WORTH it. I'M...too sexy for my SHIRT...too sexy for my LIPS...too sexy for my HAIR...

Mom: And the VIOLENCE in those TV shows and video games and movies! How do you know it won't influence you to be violent YOURSELF?

Randy: You've got NOTHIN' on ME, copper! It's only a MOVIE. Parental discretion is advised.

Mom: You see what I MEAN? Everything you say is from a SONG or a TV SHOW or a VIDEO GAME or a MOVIE!

Randy: But that's OK—because I'm GOOD ENOUGH, I'm SMART ENOUGH, and doggone it, people LIKE me!

Mom: This is getting nowhere. Randy, what's going to BECOME of you? What do you want to DO with your life?

Randy: To BOLDLY GO where no one has gone BEFORE. I'd like to teach the world to SING in perfect HARMONY.

Mom: All right, Randy. I can see that your problem is WORSE than I THOUGHT. I guess you need PROFESSIONAL help.

Randy: MAD, am I? I'LL show you who's MAD! I'll show them ALL! (*Laughs like a maniac.*)

Mom: I'm going to call the PASTOR and see if he can recommend a good COUNSELOR.

Randy: Call NOW! Operators are STANDING BY!

Mom: I'm going. I hope you'll THINK about what I've said.

Randy: HASTA LA VISTA, baby. You've made me so very happy; I'm so GLAD you came into my life. LIFE is like a BOX of CHOCOLATES. Member FDIC. Some RESTRICTIONS may apply. Your mileage may VARY. See DEALER for DETAILS. That's ALL, folks! This program was taped before a LIVE AUDIENCE.

(**Mom** *exits, shaking her head.*)

Randy: MAN! What was SHE so bothered about? (*Turns stereo and TV back on, then stares blankly at TV.*) We NOW return to our regularly scheduled PROGRAMMING.

For Post-Play Pondering:

1. Do you think adults worry too much, too little, or just the right amount about how music, movies, and other entertainment might affect you?

2. Are you for or against the following: "explicit language" warning labels on music, sex-and-violence ratings on movies, "parental discretion" warnings before TV shows, and violence ratings on video games? Why?

3. If you were a parent, would you want your teenager to watch and listen to all the things you watch and listen to? Why or why not?

4. Have you ever seen a movie that you think Jesus would have walked out of? Have you ever listened to an album that you think Jesus would have turned off? Explain.

5. Which of the Ten Commandments (see Exodus 20:2-17) do you think apply most to choosing entertainment? Why?

Other Scriptures for Study:

Job 31:1-4; Psalm 119:33-37; 2 Corinthians 4:18; Ephesians 5:3-16.

The Exam

Topic: Cheating

Scripture for Study:
Proverbs 11:1-6

The Scene: A waiting room

The Simple Setup: You'll need two chairs and two real or imagined doorways. You'll also need a homemade "eye chart" for **Kyle** to put in his pocket. Create the chart using the following pattern: The first and largest row of letters on the chart should be: E, H, T. The second row should be smaller than the first and include: G, Y, F, N. The third row should be smaller than the second and include: Q, C, I, B, Z. The fourth row should be smaller than the third and include: R, D, O, L, M, P. The letters should be bold enough for the audience to see. **Kyle** should be played by a group member who isn't wearing glasses. If you prefer, **Kyle** and **Gordon** could be played by girls, with appropriate name changes.

Other Options: The **Receptionist** could carry a clipboard and wear a white lab-type coat or uniform similar to one that might be worn in a doctor's office.

The Characters:
   Kyle Weatherby, an overly confident student
   Gordon, his friend
   Receptionist, a young woman who is friendly but professional

(**Gordon** sits on a chair, looking bored. **Kyle** enters and sits next to him.)

Gordon: KYLE! How did your big EXAM go? Do you think you PASSED?

Kyle: PASSED? Man, I ACED it!

Gordon: How can you be so SURE?

Kyle: Well…(*Leans toward* **Gordon**.) Can you keep a SECRET?

Gordon: I GUESS so.

Kyle: I got by with a little help from my FRIEND here. (*Taps his shirt pocket.*) I had a COPY of the TEST. (*Pulls just enough of the paper out of his pocket so that* **Gordon** *can see it, then puts it back.*) I MEMORIZED it.

Gordon: You mean you got a COPY of the test BEFOREHAND? That's CHEATING!

Kyle: Keep your VOICE down, man! Anyway, what's the big DEAL?

Go: Cheating is WRONG, Kyle!

Kyle: Oh, YEAH? Who SAYS?

Gordon: The BIBLE. People at CHURCH ... YOU know.

Kyle: EVERYBODY cheats, Gordo. Did you ever GLANCE AROUND during a big exam? So many kids have ANSWERS written on their ARMS, they look like they just came from a TATTOO PARLOR.

Gordon: But cheating is like STEALING. You're STEALING a score you don't DESERVE. And you stole that TEST you copied.

Kyle: So WHAT? I can't afford to blow an exam like THIS one. I've got to use every trick I can THINK of.

Gordon: (Sighing) SO, when will you find out how you DID?

Kyle: It should be any MINUTE now. Somebody's supposed to come out and TELL me.

Gordon: I STILL think you shouldn't have cheated. You're just hurting YOURSELF, you know.

Kyle: Oh, yeah, RIGHT. By getting a better score, I'm hurting myself. THAT makes sense.

Gordon: Maybe you NEED to know your real score. Maybe it would be low, and with a little help you could make up the DIFFERENCE. Maybe you really need to KNOW the stuff on this test to get along LATER in life.

Kyle: Oh, I'm SURE! Here, take a LOOK at my copy of the test. (*Pulls paper from his pocket, unfolds it, and holds it so that Gordon and the audience can see that it's an eye-exam chart.*) See THIS?

Gordon: Yeah.

Kyle: Read it out LOUD.

Gordon: E...H...T...G...Y...F...N...Q...C...I...B...Z...R...D...
O...L...M...P.

Kyle: And what does THAT spell?

Gordon: NOTHING.

Kyle: EXACTLY! This test doesn't even make SENSE!

Gordon: But ...

Kyle: I'M not going to need this stuff later in life! It's POINTLESS!

Gordon: But ...

Kyle: So I might as well cheat. It doesn't HURT anybody—especially not
ME!

(The **Receptionist** enters.)

Receptionist: Kyle Weatherby?

(**Kyle** scrambles to stuff the paper into his pocket and look innocent.)

Kyle: Yes? Right HERE!

Receptionist: I have the results of your EXAM. Your score was PERFECT. Your
VISION is TWENTY/TWENTY. So you won't need GLASSES after all.

Kyle: All RIGHT!

Receptionist: You can GO now. We'll see you NEXT year. (Exits.)

(**Kyle** and **Gordon** stand up.)

Kyle: This is GREAT! I'd HATE to wear glasses!

Gordon: YEAH, but ...

Kyle: Let's go CELEBRATE. I want a DOUBLE BACON CHEESEBURGER and a SHAKE. No, TWO shakes.

Gordon: I STILL think you shouldn't have cheated. You're just hurting YOUR-SELF. (*Exits.*)

Kyle: Man, what are you TALKING about? (*He tries to exit but bumps into the wall.*) OW! I'm not HURTING myself! (*Tries again to exit but walks into the wall again.*) OW! Where did they move that DOOR? (*Feels his way along the wall to the doorway.*) Hey, wait for ME!

For Post-Play Pondering:

1. How could cheating on the following exams hurt the cheater or others: a test for paramedics, a driving test, a drug test for a nuclear-power plant employee, a spelling test, a pre-football physical, and an algebra test?

2. Has anyone ever cheated you out of anything? How did you feel? How would you react to someone who said, "Hey, there's nothing wrong with cheating. Everybody does it"?

3. Which of the following factors do you think causes most of the cheating in your school: pressure from parents, fear of not getting into college, fear of not getting a good job, laziness, peer pressure, or others?

4. Is cheating most like lying, stealing, envying, or is it like all of these? Explain.

5. If everyone's cheating in school were automatically revealed when the cheaters reached age 21, how might study habits change? If you believe people's sins will be uncovered after they die, should it affect your attitude toward cheating? Does it?

Other Scriptures for Study:

Exodus 18:21; Luke 16:10-12; 19:1-9; 1 Corinthians 6:7-11.

The Initiation

Topic: Accepting One Another

Scripture for Study:
1 Peter 4:7-11

The Scene: A church youth group's meeting place

The Simple Setup: Three chairs are needed for the Committee. These should be set up behind a long, sturdy table. The chairs and table should be angled so that while the three pledges stand in front of the table, the Committee can still be seen. Props (the weights and the rack handles) should be pantomimed.

Other Options: Those on the Committee could be dressed in clothes that mark them as socially elite in your area.

The Characters:
> **Acceptance Committee Chairman**, a discriminating student leader
> **Committee Member One**, a very proper girl
> **Committee Member Two**, a very snooty guy
> **Pledge A**, a nervous girl
> **Pledge B**, a nervous guy
> **Pledge C**, a nervous girl

▲ ▲ ▲ ▲ ▲ ▲ ▲ ▲

*(The **Chairman** and **Members** of the Committee are seated behind a long table. The **Pledges** stand in front of the table, facing the Committee.)*

Chairman: Ladies and gentlemen, let us begin our YOUTH GROUP INITIATION CEREMONY. As the ACCEPTANCE COMMITTEE, our job is to WEED OUT those who don't BELONG here. That's best for EVERYONE.

Members One and Two: *(Together)* Of COURSE.

Chairman: Will the FIRST PLEDGE approach the committee? (**Pledge A** *takes a step toward the Committee.*) On your HANDS AND KNEES, please. (**Pledge A** *gets down and crawls toward the Committee.*) NAME?

Pledge A: Delores Bloomfield.

**Members
One and Two:** (*Together*) We don't LIKE that name.

Chairman: Very well. From now on your name will be CAITLIN SUMMERS.

**Members
One and Two:** (*Together*) Ooh, we LIKE that.

Chairman: Pledge Caitlin Summers, you must prove yourself WORTHY of our group by CARRYING THE WEIGHT OF OUR EXPECTATIONS!

(**Members One** and **Two**, as they list the following expectations, pile heavy objects in **Pledge A's** arms, who struggles with their weight.)

Member One: You must be FRIENDLY. (*Adds a weight.*)

Member Two: But not TOO friendly. (*Adds another weight.*)

Member One: Be ATHLETIC. (*Adds another weight.*)

Member Two: But NOT a JOCK. (*Adds another weight.*)

Member One: Wear the right CLOTHES. (*Adds another weight.*)

Member Two: But DON'T look better than I do. (*Adds another weight.*)

(**Pledge A** tries to carry the weights but makes it only a few steps.)

Pledge A: UGGGHHH! (*She collapses to the floor.*)

Member One: (*Taking the pulse of* **Pledge A**) She's DEAD.

Chairman: Hmm. Too bad. NEXT! (*The* **Members** *sit down.* **Pledge B** *gets down and crawls toward the Committee.*) NAME?

Pledge B: Jerome Johnson.

**Members
One and Two:** (*Together*) We don't LIKE that name.

Chairman: Very well. From now on your name will be CHAD WHITTINGTON THE THIRD.

**Members
One and Two:** (*Together*) OOH!

Chairman: Pledge Chad Whittington the Third, you must PROVE yourself WORTHY of our group by surviving the STRETCHING RACK!

(**Pledge B** *lies on the table.* **Members** **One** *and* **Two**, *as they list the following rules, pretend to turn handles at each end of the table and "stretch"* **Pledge B**.)

Member One: You must STRETCH to FIT OUR GROUP. (*Turns a handle.*)

Pledge B: OWWW!

Member Two: You must stretch to REACH OUT TO OTHERS. (*Turns a handle.*)

Pledge B: AARRGHH!

Member One: But don't expect anyone to reach out to YOU. (*Turns a handle.*)

Pledge B: YOW!

Member Two: You must LET YOURSELF BE PULLED IN ALL DIRECTIONS, trying to please EVERYONE. (*Turns a handle.*)

Pledge B: AAUUGHH! (*He collapses.*)

Member Two: Oops.

Member One: (*Taking the pulse of* **Pledge B**) HE'S dead, too.

Chairman: A pity. NEXT! (*The* **Members** *sit down.*) NAME?

Pledge C: Maria Valdez. And I'm OUTTA here! (*Exits.*)

Member One: UH-oh.

Member Two: She's not DEAD.

Member One: But she's GONE. And we didn't get to do the OBSTACLE COURSE.

Chairman: HUMPH! Who does she think she IS? NEXT!

Member One: (*After a pause*) There ISN'T anybody else.

Member Two: Well, THIS initiation went pretty much like the LAST one. And the one before THAT. And the one before THAT.

Chairman: As chairman of the Committee, I hereby declare this meeting adjourned. BUFFY...JORDAN...see you later. (*Exits.*)

Member One: (*After a pause*) I wonder why our group never gets any BIGGER.

Member Two: Search ME. It's always the same three people—US! (*They exit.*)

For Post-Play Pondering:

1. When you first came to our group, did you sense that people were "looking you over" and deciding whether you were "OK"? If so, how did you feel about that?

2. What are three unwritten expectations we tend to have of people in our group? What are two ways in which we expect them to "stretch"? What's one obstacle we tend to throw in the path of new members?

3. Why do some groups (sororities, fraternities, and so on) have initiation ceremonies? Why don't most church youth groups?

4. Is becoming a Christian like going through an initiation? Why or why not? What kind of "Acceptance Committee Chairman" would God make? Why?

5. If you had to invent an initiation ceremony that helped everyone in our group feel accepted instead of rejected, what would it be like?

Other Scriptures for Study:

Deuteronomy 10:16-19; Romans 15:1-7; 3 John 5-6.

Heaven Can Wait

Topic: Heaven

Scripture for Study:
Revelation 19:5-9; 22:1-5

The Scene: A room

The Simple Setup: Two chairs and one entrance are needed. If you wish, you could make the characters female by changing the names and a few words of dialogue.

Other Options: **Ben** and **Taylor** could be dressed in white hospital-type gowns or similar apparel. The **Technician** could wear a white lab-type coat.

The Characters:
    Ben, a teenage guy
    Taylor, his friend
    Technician, a friendly but professional man

▲ ▲ ▲ ▲ ▲ ▲ ▲ ▲

(**Ben** and **Taylor** sit on chairs, unconscious. **Ben** starts to wake up.)

Ben: Uhhh. Wha—what's going ON? (*He looks over, sees* **Taylor**, *and shakes him.*)TAYLOR! Wake UP!

Taylor: Where…where AM I?BEN! What are YOU doing here?

Ben: Why are we dressed in these WHITE ROBES?

Taylor: What IS this place?

Ben: Well…we were in the CAR, right?

Taylor: YOU were DRIVING, and we hit that patch of ICE…

Ben: The car spun out of CONTROL, we hit the TREE, and…

Taylor: Everything went BLACK.

Ben: And now we're sitting in a SPOTLESS, WHITE ROOM, wearing WHITE ROBES.

Taylor: UH-oh. We're in...

Ben and Taylor: (*Together*) HEAVEN!

Taylor: Ben, we died and went to HEAVEN! Just like we learned in CHURCH all those years!

Ben: Oh, NO! It's going to be so...

Ben and Taylor: (*Together*) BORING!

Ben: Oh, MAN! It's already like we THOUGHT it would be!

Taylor: Just SITTING AROUND doing NOTHING!

Ben: And looking really STUPID in these WHITE ROBES!

Taylor: Soon somebody will come and GET us and make us SING in a big CHOIR!

Ben: For the next ONE THOUSAND YEARS!

Taylor: THOUSAND? You mean a MILLION!

Ben: MILLION? You mean GAZILLION! This is ETERNITY! Like FOREVER!

Taylor: I just KNEW it would be like this! I didn't want to go to, YOU know, the OTHER place. But I didn't really want to go HERE, either.

Ben: There's nothing to DO! No VIDEO GAMES! No TV! No SOFTBALL!

Taylor: No TACO CHIPS!

Ben: Just MANSIONS and stuff. It's like *The* TWILIGHT *Zone*!

Taylor: Maybe we'll get a SECOND CHANCE. Like, we'll have to go back to EARTH and do a GOOD DEED to EARN OUR WINGS or something.

Ben: WINGS? Man, that's only in the MOVIES. The BIBLE says each person dies ONCE, and that's IT. And if you're a CHRISTIAN, you go to HEAVEN.

Taylor: We WERE, and here we ARE.

Ben and Taylor: (*Together*) And we HATE it!

(The **Technician** *enters.*)

Technician: AH! I see you're AWAKE. That's GOOD.

Ben: PLEASE don't make us join the CHOIR!

Taylor: We can't SING!

Technician: SING? You boys really DID bump your heads in that car accident!

Ben: Bump our HEADS? We did a lot worse than THAT!

Taylor: YEAH! Otherwise, why would we be HERE?

Technician: Well, you're here to get X-RAYS.

Ben: X-RAYS?

Technician: RIGHT. To make sure you didn't break any BONES.

Taylor: Uh...your name isn't GABRIEL or anything like that, is it?

Technician: No. It's JEFF. I'm an X-RAY TECHNICIAN.

Ben: And where ARE we?

Technician: At Memorial HOSPITAL. Where did you THINK you were?

Ben and Taylor:		(*Together*) Uhhh…(*They look at each other.*) In…THE HOSPITAL!
Taylor:		WE knew that!
Technician:		OK. Can you both WALK?
Ben and Taylor:		SURE! (*They get up and do a few martial arts moves.*)
Ben:		We're FINE—NOW!
Technician:		Then follow ME. (*Exits.*)
Ben:		(*To* **Taylor**) Boy, that was a CLOSE one!
Taylor:		I'LL say! (*Pauses.*) Do you think heaven really WILL be like this?
Ben:		I don't know. But let's not find out for a LONG, LONG TIME!

(*They exit.*)

For Post-Play Pondering:

1. What did the characters in this skit assume about heaven? What do you assume about it?

2. How would you describe heaven to a five year old? to someone your age who is really into sports? to an elderly person who has terminal cancer?

3. Would you rather go to heaven when you die or just cease to exist? Why?

4. Without mentioning fire, how would you describe the three biggest differences between heaven and hell?

5. From what you know about God, how would you feel about spending eternity with him? What five questions would you most like to ask him about heaven?

Other Scriptures for Study:

John 14:1-4; Romans 8:18-25; 1 Corinthians 2:9-10; Philippians 3:12-21.

Iron Will

Topic: Temptation

Scripture for Study:
James 1:12-15

The Scene: Under a tree at a school

The Simple Setup: No set is needed. Lunch sacks will be needed by **Greg**, **Leeza**, and **Clark**. Other props should be pantomimed. Note that **Leeza** and **Clark** should speak without much emotion, but not in a complete monotone or like robots—so that the ending isn't revealed too soon. You or a helper should provide the offstage clanging sound at the end.

Other Options: **Leeza** and **Clark** could use empty plastic "sports bottles" for their "brake fluid." You might also make sure that their appearance is as "perfect" as possible—hair combed, clothes neat, and so on.

The Characters:

> **Greg**, an average student
> **Leeza**, a "perfect" student
> **Clark**, another "perfect" student
> **Tempter A**, a sneaky, sleazy guy
> **Tempter B**, a sneaky, sleazy student (male or female)

(*Greg is sitting under the tree, starting to open his lunch sack when **Leeza** and **Clark** enter—also carrying sacks.*)

Leeza: HELLO. We could not help noticing you under this TREE, starting to eat your LUNCH.

Clark: May we JOIN you? I am CLARK, and this is LEEZA. (*Leeza and Clark sit next to Greg.*) We are new at school.

Greg: I'm GREG. (*Clark and Leeza suddenly bow their heads as if praying.*) Hello? (*They raise their heads and open their eyes.*) Are you guys OK?

Leeza: We were ASKING THE BLESSING. Are you UNFAMILIAR with this practice?

Greg: NO! As a matter of fact, I'm a Christian MYSELF. But I feel SILLY praying in PUBLIC. I guess I'm just WEAK.

*(**Tempter A** enters and waves a magazine under **Clark's** nose.)*

Tempter A: HEY, guys! Did you see the latest issue of PLAYBOY magazine? Take a look at this CENTERFOLD!

*(**Greg** cranes his neck to see it, but **Clark** turns away.)*

Clark: We are not INTERESTED. You should look at a CHRISTIAN magazine.

Tempter A: What a LOSER! (*Exits.*)

Greg: WOW! How'd you look away from a tempting picture like THAT?

Clark: I simply rotated my head at a forty-degree angle. Can YOU do that?

Greg: (*Sighing*) Yeah, I GUESS so. But it's TOUGH!

*(**Tempter B** enters.)*

Tempter B: HI! Some of us are having a PARTY tonight on the BEACH. There'll be plenty of FREE BEER. Wanna GO?

Leeza: Sorry, but underage drinking is ILLEGAL.

Clark: And DRUNKENNESS is prohibited in SCRIPTURE.

Tempter B: Talk about WEIRD! (*Exits.*)

Greg: Weren't you guys even a LITTLE tempted to go to that party?

Leeza: Of COURSE not. How could ANYONE be tempted by POPULARITY and FUN?

Greg: I guess there's something WRONG with me.

*(**Tempters A** and **B** enter together.)*

Tempter A: HEY! Want some CHEWING tobacco? X-rated VIDEOS?

Tempter B: How about a little VANDALISM? or SKIPPING CHURCH? or breaking into the school COMPUTER system and giving yourself STRAIGHT A'S?

Clark: We find NONE of those things appealing.

Leeza: We would rather participate in WHOLESOME activities.

Tempters: (*Together*) That's TWISTED! (**Tempters A** *and* **B** *exit.*)

Greg: Aren't you guys tempted by ANYTHING?

Leeza: No. We are IN this world but not OF it.

Greg: Not of this world? Are you ... ALIENS?

Clark: (*With a fake-sounding laugh*) NO, NO. We are not aliens.

Greg: Sorry. I've just never seen anybody who was so GOOD at resisting temptation! (*Pauses.*) Anyway, let's have lunch. (*Opens his lunch sack.*) I've got a roast beef sandwich. What have YOU got?

Leeza: (*Opening her sack*) BRAKE FLUID.

Clark: (*Opening his sack*) As do I.

Greg: BRAKE FLUID? What kind of food is THAT?

Clark: We have no NEED of food.

Leeza: We have only to refill our HYDRAULIC PRESSURE SYSTEMS twice a day.

Greg: HYDRAULIC PRESSURE SYSTEMS? But that doesn't sound ... HUMAN!

Clark: We are NOT human. We are ANDROIDS.

Leeza: We are MODEL CHRISTIAN YOUNG PEOPLE. Model SEVEN-A and Model TWELVE-B.

(*Leeza* and *Clark* pretend to pour bottles of brake fluid into their ears.)

Clark and Leeza: (*Together*) Mmm. BRAKE FLUID.

Greg: So THAT'S why you weren't tempted by anything!

Clark: We are NOT SWAYED by temptation. We are INCAPABLE of WEAKNESS.

Greg: (*Standing*) Well, I hope you don't mind if I eat lunch somewhere ELSE. It's too DEPRESSING to be around people who are so...PERFECT! (*Exits.*)

Leeza: Foolish human. ANYONE can stand up to TEMPTATION.

Clark: All it takes is...an IRON WILL! (*Each knocks on his or her head twice as an offstage helper provides a clanging sound by striking a metal pan with a spoon. Then* **Leeza** *and* **Clark** *both exit.*)

For Post-Play Pondering:

1. What was your first clue that Leeza and Clark weren't "normal"? Do you think it's more normal to resist temptation or to give in to it? Why?

2. Why do you suppose God doesn't take away our weaknesses when we become Christians? How would your life be different if he did?

3. Which of the temptations mentioned in this skit would have no appeal to you? What advice could you give to someone who does find those temptations appealing?

4. Is temptation usually more like (a) a sneaky person who walks up to you, (b) a little voice inside your head, (c) a growling in your stomach, or (d) something else?

5. If God is a forgiving God as Scripture promises, why do you suppose he wants us to resist temptation in the first place?

6. Do you think an "iron will" was what enabled Jesus to resist all temptation? How do you think he feels about the way you handle temptation?

7. What are Christians to do when we've "blown it" and given into temptation? (See 1 John 1:9). What will God do in response? What does this mean to you personally?

Other Scriptures for Study:

Genesis 39; Matthew 4:1-11; 1 Corinthians 10:12-13.

Lords of the Mall

The Scene: A shopping mall

The Simple Setup: No set is needed. Props may be pantomimed. The **Guards** may be played by guys or girls.

Other Options: Use toy walkie-talkies as props if you wish. The **Guards** could wear dark blue clothing with badge-shaped patches taped to the shoulders. The **Supervisor** could wear a dress shirt, tie, and slacks.

The Characters:

    Guard One, an unimpressive but tough-talking mall security guard
    Guard Two, another unimpressive but tough-talking mall security guard
    Guard Three, a mall security guard who tries to serve others
    Supervisor, kind but firm boss of the other three

(**Guard One** *stands alone, peering suspiciously at unseen mallgoers, then puts a walkie-talkie next to his or her mouth.*)

One: Uh, this is MALL SECURITY SECTOR SEVEN, over. I was just down in the RESTROOM. We've got a MAJOR OVERFLOW SITUATION. Request BACKUP. No, CANCEL that. Already HAVE backup. Need somebody to UNCLOG backup. Over.

(**Guard Two** *enters.*)

Two: So, how's it GOING?

One: HARD DAY. The snack bar ran out of PRETZELS—the BIG ones with the ROCK SALT on 'em.

Two: Yeah, that SALT toughens you UP. You've GOTTA be tough in THIS job!

One: You're telling ME! Malls are FULL of DANGEROUS CRIMINALS!

Two: (Calling to unseen visitor) Hey, LADY! You can't take PICTURES of the FOUNTAIN! (Speaks into a walkie-talkie.) This is mall security sector seven. We've got a possible SHUTTERBUG proceeding SOUTHWEST at POINT-ZERO-ONE miles per hour. Be on the LOOKOUT. Over.

One: CIVILIANS! The mall would be a better place WITHOUT 'em. (Pauses, then calls to unseen visitor.) Hey, YOU! You've been on that bench for THREE-POINT-EIGHT MINUTES! That's LOITERING! MOVE ALONG before I THROW YOU OUT!

Two: HEY, look who's coming this way. That NEW GUARD from SECTOR FIVE.

One: What a WIMP! He doesn't understand what mall security is all ABOUT. Thinks this is some kind of CHARITY or something.

(**Guard Three** enters.)

Three: HI! What's UP?

Two: Can't TALK about it. Let's just say we've been on the RADIO a lot. Using CODE WORDS and that kind of stuff. (Pauses, then calls to unseen visitor.) Hey, YOU! Little GIRL! Quit that CRYING!

Two: YEAH! I can hardly hear the MUZAK!

Three: Oh, she's LOST. (To unseen girl) Honey, where's your MOMMY? Is THAT her in the green dress? HERE she comes. YOU'RE OK now. (To unseen mother) No PROBLEM, ma'am. Have a nice day.

One: EEEW! I think I'm gonna BARF!

Two: (To **Three**) You're a DISGRACE to the UNIFORM!

One: You've got to command RESPECT! Like THIS! (Pauses, then calls to unseen visitor.) YOU there! Old MAN! Get off the FLOOR!

Three: But he FELL DOWN! (To unseen old man) Are you all RIGHT? Is this YOUR cane? (Hands imaginary cane to unseen old man.) You just REST. I'll radio for a WHEELCHAIR.

One: A WHEELCHAIR? He doesn't need a WHEELCHAIR! (*To unseen old man*) Get UP, you lazy old coot!

Two: One more minute in that spot, and you'll be LOITERING!

Three: (*Speaking into a walkie-talkie*) This is mall security sector seven. Could you send a wheelchair? We have an elderly man who needs HELP. Over.

One: OOH, you're in trouble NOW!

Two: YEAH! You're only supposed to use the radio for EMERGENCIES! Like when you find a CANDY WRAPPER on the floor and you need one of those dumb JANITORS to come pick it up.

Three: Why not pick it up YOURSELF?

Two: What AM I, a SLAVE?

One: We're HIGHLY-TRAINED SECURITY PROFESSIONALS!

Two: Whoa, LOOK! Here comes the BOSS!

One: (*To* **Three**) Better get ready to TURN IN YOUR BADGE!

(The **Supervisor** enters.)

Supervisor: I understand there was a RADIO request for a WHEELCHAIR.

One and Two: (*Together*) WE didn't do it!

Supervisor: I KNOW. (*To* **Three**) That was GOOD THINKING. I've been impressed with your work since you STARTED. I'm PROMOTING you to TAKE CHARGE of sectors FOUR THROUGH EIGHT.

One: But ...

Supervisor: As for YOU two, I'd suggest you pay more attention to the needs of our VISITORS and less attention to PRETZELS. If you want to be GREAT IN SECURITY, learn to be a SERVANT OF ALL.

One:  SERVANT!?

Supervisor: You can start by unclogging that TOILET in the RESTROOM.

One and Two: (*Together*) TOILET? GROSS! (*They exit.*)

Supervisor: Well, that man has his wheelchair now. Come with me to sector FOUR. We've got some HIGH-LEVEL WORK to do.

Three: HIGH-LEVEL, sir?

Supervisor: The HIGHEST. Scraping CHEWING GUM off the bottoms of the BENCHES.

Three: Yes, SIR! (*They exit.*)

For Post-Play Pondering:

1. What's the worst chore you've ever had to do? Why did you do it? How did you feel when you did it? What could have made you feel better about it?

2. How would you rank the following titles in order of "most respectable" to "least respectable": servant, employee, helper, aide, slave, assistant, gofer, flunkie, right-hand person? Why?

3. How would you change this skit if it took place in our group instead of in a mall?

4. What was Jesus' "payment" for the servant-like work he did for us on the cross? What is our payment for being his servants?

5. What four people are in a position to "lord it over" you if they want to? Do they? What two people could you "lord it over" if you wanted to? Do you? What act of serving could you perform for those two people this week that would most surprise them?

6. What do you think Jesus meant when he taught that true greatness means being a servant to others?

Other Scriptures for Study:
Proverbs 16:18-19; 17:2; John 13:1-17; Philippians 2:3-11.

Wholly Moses

Topic: Faith

Scripture for Study:
Hebrews 11

The Scene: A palace in ancient Egypt

The Simple Setup: Place two chairs for **Moses** and **Aaron** on one side of the stage and a third chair representing a throne on the other side. Angle all of the chairs so that the audience can see the actors' faces during the meeting with **Pharaoh**. You'll also need two entrances (one for **Moses** and **Aaron**, one for **Pharaoh** and the **Guard**).

Other Options: Period costumes (robes, a cardboard "King Tut" headdress for **Pharaoh**, and a broom-handle spear for the **Guard**) would help to identify the characters and setting.

The Characters:
> **Moses**, nervous leader of the Israelites
> **Aaron**, his sensible brother
> **Pharaoh**, hard-hearted ruler of Egypt
> **Guard**, a casual and forgetful guy

*(The **Guard** enters on the throne side. **Moses** and **Aaron** enter from the opposite side.)*

Guard: Enter the palace of the GREAT AND MIGHTY PHARAOH, RULER of all EGYPT, and ... SOMETHING of the DESERT. CACTUS of the desert?

Moses: I think it's LION of the desert.

Guard: Oh, right. Thanks. I take it you've BEEN here before.

Aaron: MANY times.

Moses: TOO many.

Guard: Then you know the ROUTINE. Have a seat. The Pharaoh will see you when he's ready. (*Exits.*)

(**Moses** and **Aaron** sit.)

Moses: Aaron, I'm NERVOUS.

Aaron: Moses, you're ALWAYS nervous. You were nervous when you saw the burning BUSH. You were nervous about getting into a CAMEL ACCIDENT on the way OVER here.

Moses: But this PLAGUE thing isn't WORKING. We've been here AGAIN and AGAIN. I keep telling Pharaoh, "Let my people GO!" And he never DOES.

Aaron: But you've got a NEW plague. What did the Lord say it would BE?

Moses: DARKNESS! All the Egyptians have to do is TURN THEIR LIGHTS ON!

Aaron: The Lord knows what he's DOING, Moses. You must have FAITH.

Moses: But we've been through so many plagues ALREADY! Did the river of BLOOD make Pharaoh let us go? did the GNATS? the BOILS? the LOCUSTS?

Aaron: No. But THAT doesn't mean...

Moses: Don't you get it? We can't COUNT ON the Lord to get us out of Egypt. We have to take matters into our OWN HANDS. I've been WORKING on it—and I've come up with a few plagues of my OWN.

Aaron: Plagues of your OWN? Moses, how are you going to...

(The **Guard** enters.)

Guard: OK. The Pharaoh will SEE you now.

(**Moses** and **Aaron** stand.)

Guard: Let ALL BOW DOWN before the GREAT AND MIGHTY PHARAOH, RULER of ... uh ... Well, YOU know.

*(The **Pharaoh** enters and sits on the throne. The **Guard** stands by the throne, and **Moses** and **Aaron** stand in front of it.)*

Pharaoh: SO! MOSES and AARON! What's it going to be THIS time? A plague of ATHLETE'S FOOT? Or will it RAIN CATS AND DOGS?

Moses: Neither ONE, mighty Pharaoh. This time, if you refuse to let my people go, I'll...SCRAPE MY FINGERS across a CHALKBOARD!

Aaron: MOSES! Stick with the LORD'S plagues!

Pharaoh: Nice TRY, Moses, but no CIGAR.

Moses: OK, Pharaoh. If you won't let us go, you'll have to...listen to some REALLY BAD MUSIC! *(Sings.)* FEELINGS...nothing more than FEELINGS...

Pharaoh: Pretty AWFUL, Moses. But you and your people are STAYING!

Aaron: EXCUSE me, O mighty Pharaoh. Moses hasn't been FEELING well lately. What he MEANS to say is that the Lord will send a plague of...

Moses: BAD HAIRCUTS! That's RIGHT! You want a plague? EVERYBODY IN EGYPT will get a REALLY BAD HAIRCUT! You'll be so...EMBARRASSED!

Pharaoh: I've heard ENOUGH. I'm NEVER going to let your people go now. If THIS is the worst your God can do, I have NO FEAR of him.

Aaron: Uh...Pharaoh, I was just WONDERING. How would you feel about THREE DAYS of total DARKNESS? I mean, SO DARK you couldn't see your HAND in front of your FACE?

Guard: Oh, he'd HATE that! He sleeps with a NIGHT LIGHT on!

Pharaoh: SILENCE, you fool! *(Stands.)* I...uh...have to be GOING. I want to make sure all the flashlights have BATTERIES in them! *(Exits.)*

Guard: I guess I shouldn't have SAID that. You're not supposed to say that about the LIAR of the DESERT.

Aaron: That's LION of the desert.

Guard: Oh, yeah. I've gotta write that DOWN. (*Exits.*)

Aaron: SEE, Moses? The LORD knows which plagues to send. The darkness will strike FEAR into Pharaoh's heart.

Moses: Yeah, but he'll CHANGE HIS MIND. He always DOES.

Aaron: Perhaps. But the Lord will bring us out of Egypt in his OWN good time. We must trust in HIS power, not our OWN.

Moses: OK! (*Starts to exit, but stops.*) I had one MORE plague, you know.

Aaron: What WAS it?

Moses: Well, you know how it hurts if you get up in the middle of the night and STUB YOUR TOE on the DRESSER or something? I was thinking we could go around and STUB ALL THE EGYPTIANS' TOES some night.

Aaron: (*Sighing*) Moses, if I were you I'd . . . PASS OVER that idea.

Moses: PASS OVER? Hm . . .

(*They exit.*)

For Post-Play Pondering:

1. Why didn't God just send one killer plague to Egypt and get it over with? If you'd been in Moses' place, how would you have felt about continuing to trust God?

2. In the following situations, what's the longest you could wait before taking things into your own hands: (a) your people are oppressed because of their race; (b) the murderer of your sister goes unpunished; and (c) your father, who has cancer, refuses to go to the doctor because he believes God has healed him? In each case, what would you want to do?

3. Of your prayers that seem to go unanswered, which one frustrates you most? How long do you think a person should pray for something before giving up?

4. How can you tell when you should pray for something, and when you should go ahead and try to make it happen yourself? Who could help you decide?

5. What would "prove" to you that God really can be trusted with every part of your life? What do you plan to do if you don't get that proof?

Other Scriptures for Study:

Exodus 3–12; Psalm 34:1-8; Zechariah 4:6; 2 Corinthians 12:7-10.

All the Answers

The Scene: The bedroom of **Brenda**, a teenager

The Simple Setup: Two chairs can represent **Brenda's** bed. **Brenda** could be changed to **Brent** if you want a guy to play the role. If you do that, be sure to alter names and dialogue as needed. Props may be pantomimed. The door may be real or imagined.

Other Options: For greater effect, the person providing the voice of **God** might speak into a live microphone. If you want to use props, you'll need a stack of books that look like college catalogs.

The Characters:
    Brenda, a confused high school girl
    God, represented by a firm but gentle offstage voice
    Mom, mother of **Brenda**

(**Brenda** *is sitting on the end of her bed, leafing through college catalogs.*)

Brenda: MAN! These COLLEGE CATALOGS are driving me NUTS! (*Picks up one catalog.*) THIS school has SCHOLARSHIPS, but no INTERNSHIPS. (*Picks up another catalog.*) THIS one has SPORTSMAN-SHIP, but no FELLOWSHIP. (*Picks up another catalog.*) THIS one just has a SHIP. (*Pauses.*) I can't make up my mind. I guess I'll have to ... PRAY. (*Bows her head.*) Dear God ... PLEASE help me know which COLLEGE I should go to. Amen. (*Lifts her head and waits a moment.*) NOTHING. You ask God what to DO, and he says NOTHING. I wish he'd COME RIGHT OUT just ONCE and SHOW me what his will is. But NO, he never says ANYTHING!

God: NEVER?

Brenda: Who SAID that?

God: It's GOD, Brenda. I've HEARD your request to know my will, and I've decided to speak to you about it DIRECTLY.

Brenda: WOW! This is GREAT! No more wondering what I should DO! So, which college should I PICK?

God: I'll GET to that. But FIRST... I believe you have some PLANS for this evening.

Brenda: Well, I'm just going to watch my favorite TV show. The one with the beach and all those guys in SWIMSUITS...

God: THAT'S not my WILL for you, Brenda. Try doing your HOMEWORK instead.

Brenda: (Sighing) Oh, all RIGHT. NOW, about choosing a COLLEGE...

God: In a moment. FIRST I'd like to hear your plans for TOMORROW.

Brenda: BUT... Well, OK. At LUNCH I'll be meeting my friends Lisa and Chris at that HOT DOG place near SCHOOL.

God: SORRY, Brenda. Every time you're WITH them, you TEAR DOWN your TEACHERS and the PRINCIPAL. I want you to RESPECT authority. My will is that you find some NEW friends.

Brenda: HEY! YOU can't tell me what to...

God: Pardon ME?

Brenda: Uh... let me REPHRASE that. If I don't eat with THOSE friends, who will I EAT with?

God: Go to the THIRD table from the back in the SCHOOL CAFETERIA. You'll find some kids who NEED your FRIENDSHIP.

Brenda: You mean the REJECTS?

God: Have LUNCH with them, Brenda. THAT'S my will for you.

Brenda: Oh, MAN. (*Pauses.*) I suppose I should forget my FIFTH PERIOD plans, TOO, right?

God: Skipping CLASS and going to see an R-rated love story is NOT my idea of a GOOD TIME.

Brenda: But it's what I LIKE!

God: MY will is that you STAY in class.

Brenda: And what about my DATE with TONY? THAT'S OK, right?

God: NO, Brenda. Tony doesn't KNOW me. You don't share the same FAITH, the same VALUES—your relationship won't LAST.

Brenda: But we've been GOING together for SIX MONTHS!

God: I KNOW. Breaking up will be HARD, but it's my WILL for you.

Brenda: Hey, LISTEN! When I said I wanted to know your WILL, I wasn't talking about this EVERYDAY stuff! I meant the BIG decisions where I can't make up my MIND!

God: Brenda…do you REALLY want to know my will or NOT?

Brenda: NO! I mean…YES. I mean…it DEPENDS.

God: On WHAT?

Brenda: On whether it agrees with MY will.

God: I SEE. That doesn't leave us much to TALK about, DOES it?

Brenda: Well…when you put it THAT way…

God: Goodbye for NOW, Brenda. I'll be around.

Brenda: WAIT! What about the COLLEGE I should go to? You didn't TELL me yet! (*Pauses.*) HEY! (*Pauses.*) HELLO! (*Pauses.*) Oh, GREAT. Now I'm right back where I STARTED.

Mom: (Offstage) BRENDA! Brenda, who are you TALKING to in there?

Brenda: Uh…NOBODY, Mom. (Stands and opens the door.) Hey, MOM?

Mom: YES, dear? (Enters and stands.)

Brenda: Where do you think I should go to COLLEGE?

Mom: It's up to YOU. Maybe you should PRAY about it. (Exits.)

(**Brenda** stares off into the audience with a look of exasperation frozen on her face.)

For Post-Play Pondering:

1. What's the last decision you had trouble making? How did you finally decide what to do?

2. If you could literally hear God talk to you for $200 a minute, how much time would you be willing to pay for each month? What would you most want him to talk about?

3. On a scale of 1 to 10 (10 being perfectly), how well have you followed what you already know of "God's will" from the Bible? Why?

4. In what two areas of your life do you feel the least need for God's guidance? Why?

5. How would you rank the effectiveness (from least to most) of these methods of getting direction from God: asking your youth leader, praying, asking a parent, reading the Bible, asking your pastor, flipping a coin, asking a non-Christian friend, opening your Bible at random and pointing to a verse with your eyes closed, and asking a Christian friend?

6. As illustrated in the skit, what types of things in your life might hinder your communication with God when you need guidance? What do you need to do about these things?

Other Scriptures for Study:

Proverbs 8:12-21; Luke 12:31; James 1:2-8.

The Gift Exchange

Topic: Spiritual gifts

Scripture for Study:
1 Corinthians 12

The Scene: The counter in a gift shop

The Simple Setup: A table can serve as the gift shop counter. All props may be pantomimed.

Other Options: If you prefer to use props, each **Customer** could carry a box "containing" his or her spiritual gift. Actors should avoid letting the audience see that the boxes are empty.

The Characters:

>**Clerk**, a polite young person
>**Customer A**, a disgusted young person
>**Customer B**, an embarrassed young person
>**Customer C**, a hurried young person
>**Customer D**, an angry young person

*(The **Clerk** is standing behind the counter. **Customer A** enters.)*

Clerk: Welcome to the SPIRITUAL GIFT SHOP. May I HELP you?

Customer A: I'm RETURNING a SPIRITUAL GIFT. It doesn't FIT me.

Clerk: But I'm sure the GIFT GIVER chose it CAREFULLY. Have you tried it ON?

Customer A: Why would I do THAT?

Clerk: To see whether it FITS.

Customer A: I can TELL it won't fit. I'd actually have to STRETCH to use this gift!

Clerk: Perhaps that's what the GIFT GIVER had in MIND.

Customer A: I don't want any gift that isn't designed to fit ME. I'm EXCHANGING it.

Clerk: I'm SORRY, but the GIFT GIVER left instructions not to ALLOW exchanges.

Customer A: Then I want a REFUND!

Clerk: Sorry, but we can only credit the GIFT GIVER'S account. If HE wants to give you ANOTHER gift, that's up to HIM.

Customer A: This is RIDICULOUS! I'm NEVER coming into this place AGAIN! (*Exits.*)

(**Customer B** *enters.*)

Clerk: Welcome to the SPIRITUAL GIFT SHOP. May I HELP you?

Customer B: I'd . . . like to RETURN a spiritual GIFT. I'd be too EMBARRASSED to use it.

Clerk: But WHY?

Customer B: Just LOOK at it! Everybody would STARE at me if I used this gift!

Clerk: But the GIFT GIVER must have WANTED you to use it.

Customer B: No WAY! I don't want to look WEIRD. Can I exchange it for something less . . . FLASHY?

Clerk: Sorry, but the GIFT GIVER said not to ALLOW exchanges. Or REFUNDS.

Customer B: Well, I'm not KEEPING it. I didn't even ASK for a spiritual gift in the FIRST place. I guess I'd rather not HAVE one at all. (*Exits.*)

(**Customer C** *enters.*)

Clerk: Welcome to the . . .

Customer C: YES, YES. I'm in a hurry. I'm returning a spiritual gift—because I already HAVE one.

Clerk: But do you have THIS one?

Customer C: No. But that doesn't MATTER. All I need is ONE.

Clerk: But I'm sure the GIFT GIVER wanted you to have ANOTHER.

Customer C: I don't WANT another! I don't have time to use the one I HAVE!

Clerk: I'm sure the GIFT GIVER KNOWS that.

Customer C: I don't have time to ARGUE. Just give me a REFUND.

Clerk: I'm sorry, but the GIFT GIVER left instructions not to . . .

Customer C: You mean I came all the way down here for NOTHING? Thanks a LOT!

(**Customer C** *starts to exit.*)

Clerk: EXCUSE me—I'm CURIOUS. What spiritual gift do you ALREADY have?

Customer C: ENCOURAGEMENT . . . you NITWIT! (*Exits.*)

(**Customer D** *enters.*)

Clerk: Welcome to the Spiritual Gift Shop. May I HELP you?

Customer D: I'm RETURNING a spiritual gift. It doesn't WORK.

Clerk: But . . . the GIFT GIVER has NEVER given ANYONE a DEFECTIVE gift.

Customer D: Well, he has NOW.

Clerk: How do you know it's BROKEN?

Customer D: I USED it—and nothing HAPPENED! It didn't make others look UP to me. It didn't make them think I'm SPIRITUAL. It didn't even make me FEEL good!

Clerk: I don't think that's what the gift giver INTENDED.

Customer D: Then why would anybody even WANT a spiritual gift?

Clerk: I believe the GIFT GIVER wants us to use our gifts to benefit OTHERS.

Customer D: That's CRAZY! Well, I guess an EXCHANGE would be pointless. It doesn't sound like ANY of your gifts would work.

Clerk: Not in the way you'd WANT them to.

Customer D: How about a REFUND?

Clerk: Sorry, but we can only credit the GIFT GIVER'S account.

Customer D: THAT figures. Well, he can KEEP his gift. NEXT time he should try giving me tickets to a HOCKEY game. Or at least a nice SWEATER! (Exits.)

Clerk: (Sighing and looking up as if to heaven) All I can say is—it's a GOOD THING You gave ME the gift of MERCY! (Exits.)

For Post-Play Pondering:

1. What reasons did the customers give for returning their spiritual gifts? How do you think God might feel about someone who wanted to "return" a spiritual gift?

2. Which of the gifts listed in 1 Corinthians 12:4-11, 28-31 do you think God would never give you? Why?

3. Why do you think God gives Christians spiritual gifts?

4. What's one question you have about spiritual gifts? What do you think the answer might be?

5. What spiritual gifts do you think people in our group have? Explain your answer.

Other Scriptures for Study:

Romans 12:3-8; 1 Corinthians 7:7; Hebrews 2:4; 1 Peter 4:10.

Hit Man

Topic: Competition

Scripture for Study:
Luke 9:23-25

The Scene: A dingy restaurant

The Simple Setup: Set two chairs on opposite sides of a table. **Melissa** and **Mr. Rudy** should wear sunglasses. Menus and plates may be pantomimed, but **Melissa** should have a real list (a long piece of paper) to produce from her purse.

Other Options: **Mr. Rudy** could wear a trench coat and a fedora hat. **Melissa** could wear an overcoat. **Vito** could have a towel draped over his arm.

The Characters:
Melissa, a student
Mr. Rudy, a middle-aged killer for hire
Vito, a young man who is a waiter

▲ ▲ ▲ ▲ ▲ ▲ ▲ ▲

(**Mr. Rudy** sits at the table, wearing sunglasses and sipping from a glass of water. **Melissa** enters hesitantly, puts on sunglasses, and sneaks to the table as if not wanting to be seen. She stands near the empty chair and speaks to **Mr. Rudy** without looking at him.)

Melissa: How much wood would a woodchuck CHUCK if a woodchuck could chuck WOOD?

Mr. Rudy: Peter Piper picked a peck of pickled PEPPERS.

Melissa: She sells SEASHELLS down by...

Mr. Rudy: Enough with the CODE words! I'm the guy you're LOOKING for!

Melissa: (Sitting) SHH! I can't afford to be SEEN with you. That's why I picked this CRUMMY little OUT-OF-THE-WAY restaurant.

(**Vito** enters.)

Vito: Mr. RUDY! Nice to SEE you again! Have you KILLED anybody lately?

Melissa:	😠	(*To* **Mr. Rudy**) HEY! Does EVERYBODY know what you do?
Mr. Rudy:	😊	Don't worry. Vito knows how to keep a SECRET. RIGHT, Vito?
Vito:	😄	SURE! (*Shouting*) Hey, LOOK, everybody! It's Mr. RUDY, the HIT man!
Mr. Rudy:	😊	THANKS, Vito. How about some MENUS?
Vito:	😊	Here you GO. (*He hands them menus.*) The SPAGHETTIOS are especially good this evening. (*Exits.*)
Melissa:	😐	Let's get to the POINT. I have . . . a JOB for you.
Mr. Rudy:	🙄	Who do you want RUBBED OUT?
Melissa:	😐	I wish you wouldn't PUT it that way.
Mr. Rudy:	🙄	OK. Who do you want MURDERED?
Melissa:	😬	SHH! Here comes the WAITER.

(**Vito** *enters.*)

Vito:	😊	SO, have you decided what you'd LIKE?
Mr. Rudy:	😊	We'll have my USUAL, Vito.
Vito:	😊	The COMBINATION platter—FRITOS and CHEETOS? EXCELLENT choice, Mr. Rudy. (*Takes the menus and exits.*)
Mr. Rudy:	🙄	You were SAYING, kid?
Melissa:	😐	I want to be NUMBER ONE. I want you to KNOCK OUT THE COMPETITION.
Mr. Rudy:	🙄	What ARE you, an OLYMPIC ICE SKATER?
Melissa:	😌	Not YET. But I'm going to be the BEST at EVERYTHING. YOUR job is to get rid of everybody who stands in my WAY.

Mr. Rudy: EVERYBODY?

Melissa: You can start with the DRAMA CLUB, SPEECH TEAM, and CHEER-LEADING SQUAD. Then the SCHOOL BAND, my HISTORY CLASS, and my competitors in the race for STUDENT-BODY PRESIDENT.

Mr. Rudy: Is that IT?

Melissa: No. Any girl who never has a BAD HAIR DAY. And the ones with more boyfriends than me. And the KIDS AT CHURCH who SING BETTER than I do.

Mr. Rudy: CHURCH? You go to CHURCH?

Melissa: Sure.

Mr. Rudy: Isn't there something in the GOOD BOOK about not MURDERING? And learning to be CONTENT with what you HAVE?

Melissa: I know that. I'm the BEST BIBLE MEMORIZER in SUNDAY SCHOOL. Except for that boy who always sits in the back row. Put HIM on the list, too, while you're at it. (*She pulls a very long piece of paper from her purse.*) Here's the list. Just TWO THOUSAND, FOUR HUNDRED THIRTY-SEVEN NAMES.

Mr. Rudy: Are you CRAZY? How are you going to PAY for all this?

Melissa: I have plenty of money saved up. I'm the BEST BABY-SITTER IN THE WORLD!

Mr. Rudy: (*Standing*) SORRY, kid. You'll have to find yourself ANOTHER hit man!

Melissa: WHY?

Mr. Rudy: I can't rub out the ENTIRE TEENAGE POPULATION in this town— even if you CAN pay for it. I may be a hired killer—but I have my STANDARDS! (*Exits.*)

(**Vito** *enters with plates of food.*)

Vito: Here you GO! (*Pauses.*) But where is Mr. Rudy?

Melissa: He...had to LEAVE.

Vito: Too bad. Well, enjoy your Fritos and Cheetos!

Melissa: (*Looking at plates*) UGH! This food looks TERRIBLE! It's got MOLD all over it! If I ATE this, I'd probably DIE of FOOD POISONING!

Vito: But ALL our food looks this way!

Melissa: HMM...that gives me an IDEA...Vito, do you think this restaurant could feed a group of my CLOSEST FRIENDS? About TWO THOUSAND, FOUR HUNDRED THIRTY-SEVEN of them?

(*They exit.*)

For Post-Play Pondering:

1. If you could knock out all your "competition" without hurting anyone, would you do it? Why or why not? How many people would have to be "gotten out of the way"?

2. Would you rather compete against others or against your own "personal best"? Why?

3. How could you tell if a student were competing "too hard" for good grades? for roles in school plays? for a football scholarship? What advice would you give that person?

4. Since God is always the "best" at everything, do you think he understands a person's drive to win and achieve? Why or why not?

5. If God had decided that people would have to compete with each other to get into heaven, what might life be like in church? in our group? Why do you suppose God didn't?

Other Scriptures for Study:

Proverbs 4:7-9; Ecclesiastes 2:22-26; 3:22; 4:4; 1 Corinthians 9:24-27.

David and the Giant

Topic: Self-Image

Scripture for Study:
1 Samuel 16:7

The Scene: King Saul's tent in the Valley of Elah

The Simple Setup: No set is needed. The door to the tent can be real or imagined. Props (armor, mirror) should be imaginary. **Goliath** stays out of sight for the entire skit. **David** must also be out of sight when he's offstage. The crash near the end of the skit can be provided by one or two offstage helpers dropping a box of pots and pans on the floor.

Other Options: Biblical costumes for all except the unseen **Goliath** would help to identify the setting. The armor still should be imaginary, however.

The Characters:
    David, ancient Israel's young hero-to-be
    Saul, king of Israel
    Soldier, the king's second-in-command
    Goliath, famous Philistine giant

(**Saul** and the **Soldier** stand in the tent.)

Soldier: KING SAUL! It's SIX O'CLOCK!

Saul: Oh, not AGAIN!

Goliath: (Offstage) Choose a man and have him come DOWN to me! If he is able to FIGHT and KILL me, we PHILISTINES will become your SLAVES. But if I kill HIM, you ISRAELITES will serve US!

Saul: He's done this for FORTY DAYS! Can't you get RID of him?

Soldier: But, sire—the men are AFRAID! Goliath is over NINE FEET TALL! His armor weighs ONE HUNDRED TWENTY-FIVE POUNDS! The iron point of his SPEAR weighs . . .

Saul: All RIGHT, all RIGHT! Enough STATISTICS!

Goliath: (*Offstage*) You COWARDS! Come out and FIGHT!

Saul: If only we could find a CHAMPION to FIGHT FOR US! Someone with SUPERNATURAL STRENGTH and COURAGE!

(**David** *knocks at the door.*)

Soldier: (*Opening the door*) Who DARES to knock at the tent of KING SAUL?

David: (*Entering*) It is I, DAVID!

Soldier: Ah, the one who's been asking about the REWARD for killing GOLIATH. But you're just a KID!

David: Your majesty, let no one lose HEART over this PHILISTINE. I'LL fight him!

Saul: YOU can't do THAT! You're only a BOY, and Goliath is a trained FIGHTING man. Not to mention the fact that he's NINE FEET TALL!

David: King Saul, GOD will PROTECT me. He helped me kill a LION and a BEAR!

Saul: 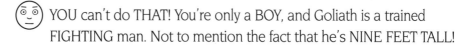 (*To* **Soldier**) Are you SURE you can't find someone else to do this?

Soldier:  We have no one over FIVE FOOT EIGHT, your majesty. And the iron point of Goliath's SPEAR alone weighs over...

Saul: ENOUGH! Very well, David. GO, and the Lord be WITH you.

David: 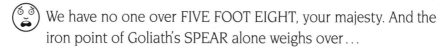 THANK you, your majesty. You won't be disappointed. I'll just get FIVE SMOOTH STONES—right after I check my hair in this MIR-ROR of yours. (*He looks into a mirror on the wall.*) Oh, NO!

Saul: What's WRONG?

David: 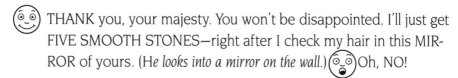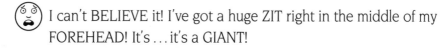 I can't BELIEVE it! I've got a huge ZIT right in the middle of my FOREHEAD! It's...it's a GIANT!

Saul: THAT'S all right. No one will NOTICE.

David: Are you KIDDING? Everybody will LAUGH at me! Why did this have to happen NOW? I can't go out there! I can't let anybody SEE me!

Goliath: (Offstage) Come ON, you Israelites! You're a bunch of SISSIES! Your king wears ARMY BOOTS!

David: WAIT! That's IT!

Soldier: WHAT'S it?

David: ARMY BOOTS! King Saul, I'll wear your ARMOR. The HELMET and EVERYTHING. That way nobody will see my giant ZIT.

Saul: But my armor is too HEAVY for you! You're not used to WEARING it!

David: I'm not leaving this tent WITHOUT it!

Saul: VERY WELL, David. Put on the armor.

*(The **Soldier** struggles to get the heavy armor on **David**. When it's on, **David** can barely move.)*

David: (Struggling) See? It's UH...a perfect FIT!

Saul: GO, David—and the Lord be WITH you!

David: (After a pause) Uh...could you help me out the DOOR? (They help him as he slowly waddles out the door.)

Saul: What a COURAGEOUS young man... I THINK.

Goliath: (Offstage) Am I a DOG that you come at me with a can of GRAVY TRAIN? What is this little SAUCEPAN that clatters toward me?

David: (Offstage) It is I, DAVID! I will STRIKE YOU DOWN and CUT OFF YOUR HEAD! I will...UH-OHHH!

(A loud, metallic crash is heard from offstage.)

Saul: DAVID! David, are you VICTORIOUS? Has GOLIATH been delivered into your HAND?

David: (Offstage) I've...FALLEN...and I CAN'T GET UP!

(**Saul** and the **Soldier** groan.)

Goliath: (Offstage) Come ON, Israelites! YOU can do better than THAT! I'll wait! I'll stand here as long as it TAKES! I'll stand here FOREVER!

Saul: (With a sigh) That's IT. I surrender. Go wave a white flag.

Soldier: As you WISH, your majesty. (Exits.)

Saul: (Looking in the mirror) Oh, GREAT! Now I'M getting one, TOO! (Exits.)

For Post-Play Pondering:

1. Why do David's actions in this skit seem silly? Does it seem silly when we try to cover up imperfections? Why or why not?

2. Which is easiest to hide: being overweight, being underweight, having acne, or having a speech impediment? Which is easiest to correct? Which is easiest to live with?

3. If you could get plastic surgery to make you look "perfect," but you'd look so different even your family wouldn't recognize you, would you do it? Why or why not?

4. If God loves you no matter how you look, why is it still hard to accept certain things about your appearance? What percentage of the world's people would have to tell you, "Wow, you're good-looking!" before you'd believe it?

5. If everyone in our group quit worrying about his or her looks for one year, how might it change the way we relate to each other? How might it change what we could accomplish?

Other Scriptures for Study:

1 Samuel 17; Isaiah 52:13-15; Matthew 10:29-31; 11:7-11.

Topics at a Glance

Scripture Index

Evaluation of *Goof-Proof Skits for Youth Ministry*

Please help Group Publishing, Inc., continue providing innovative and usable resources for ministry by taking a moment to fill out and send us this evaluation. Thanks!

● ● ●

1. As a whole, this book has been (circle one)

Not much help   Very helpful

1   2   3   4   5   6   7   8   9   10

2. The things I liked best about this book were:

3. This book could be improved by:

4. One thing I'll do differently because of this book is:

5. Optional Information:

Name_____

Street Address _____

City _____ State _____ Zip _____

Phone Number _____ Date_____

Your Teenagers Need **Real** Hope...
Real Help...**Real** Answers...
So Give Them **Real Life Bible Curriculum**™

At last—hard-hitting, biblical, *one-session* topical studies for both your senior high *and* junior high/middle school students! Now you can...
- •respond fast when kids bring up hot topics...
- •have solid, biblical answers on hand for kids' tough questions...
- •help teenagers discover for themselves what the Bible says...and
- •give your group a balanced Bible overview!

Real Life—One Point.

Each **Real Life** study zeros in on one powerful, life-changing point—in-depth. And teenagers *apply* what the Bible teaches. Every activity...discussion...decision...drives home your lesson's biblical point—and challenges teenagers to respond.

Real Life—One Price.

Every lesson is the same low price. Add a few items from your home or classroom, and you have *everything* you need for *any* size class. No student books are required.

Topics include...

Junior High/Middle School:

But God Never Leaves: How God and Friends Can Bring Comfort in Times of Hurt   1-55945-533-0
The Case of the Empty Tomb   1-55945-527-6
Fear Not!: Helping Kids Face Life With Courage   1-55945-535-7
Feeling Guilty: The Private Burden Kids Can't Shake   1-55945-422-9
I Would Die for You: Why Kids Stay in Gangs   1-55945-417-2
Kids' Deepest Need: How Jesus Fills the Void in Kids' Lives   1-55945-540-3
Listen Up: Learning to Hear God's Answers to Prayer   1-55945-415-6
The Making of the Bible   1-55945-419-9
Never Alone: God's Ultimate Answer to Loneliness   1-55945-536-5
Personal Power   1-55945-525-X
Stairways to Heaven?: The Many Ways Kids Try to Reach God   1-55945-544-6
Too-Cool Kids: Survival Tactics of a Hurting Generation   1-55945-412-1
Why Do Bad Things Happen to Me?   1-55945-531-4

Senior High:

Buddha & Mohammed—Why Not?: The Awesome Impact of Jesus' Life on Earth   1-55945-526-8
The Diary of Teenage Runaways   1-55945-530-6
Dying to Live: The Messages of Kids Who Kill Themselves   1-55945-411-3
Jesus: Myth vs. Reality   1-55945-423-7
Jesus the Rebel   1-55945-414-8
Media Seduction: The Hi-Tech Battle for the Soul of a Generation   1-55945-413-X
No Pain, No Gain: How Painful Times Can Deepen Faith in God   1-55945-418-0
Sex Worth Waiting For: Learning to Treasure God's Powerful Gift   1-55945-528-4
Taking a Stand: Motivating Young People to Stand Up for Christ   1-55945-416-4
Teenage Romance: Positive Ways to Deal With the Ups and Downs of Relationships   1-55945-529-2
To Be God...or Godly?: The Quest for True Spirituality   1-55945-539-X
Understanding Why Churches Differ   1-55945-541-1
When Friends Fight: Helping Kids Resolve Conflict   1-55945-420-2
When God Seems Silent   1-55945-532-2

...and many more!